Reading

Step by step

by
Mona McNee

A day-by-day programme of intensive systematic phonics suitable for all:

- Pre-school children
- Infants
- Remedial
- Adults
- Dyslexics

Fits in well with speech therapy.

ISBN 0 9515794 0 1

Published by Mona McNee
2 The Crescent
Toftwood
East Dereham, Norfolk

Printed by Studioprint, Rash's Green, Dereham, Norfolk

Contents

Foreword

YOU CAN teach your own child to read.

Teaching children, or adults, to read is simple and does not take long. You do not need any special training, just common sense. You start at the beginning with letters/sounds. The pupil learns how to sound out, how to join three sounds into a word, how to make c-a-t into cat, then longer words. This is the most important part; and when a child can read words like comic, hundred, this is the first third of learning to read. You know exactly where you are up to, and what the next task is. It is all fun and very exciting.

This way of teaching is called phonics. Instead of learning how to 'recognise' whole words first, the pupil learns the bits and how to put them together. The National Curriculum barely mentions phonics -- just two words: 'phonic cues', yet only on a foundation of intensive, systematic phonics will the National Curriculum work.

The second third of learning to read is to learn those sounds for which we use two or more letters, sh as in fish, aw as in crawl, and so on.

The final third is gaining fluency, and this comes from reading, practice.

Reading to and with children is a pleasant family activity, but it is not the same thing as teaching them HOW to read. Teaching reading is phonics; phonics is teaching children how to read. Many children just cannot start on whole words. Phonics gives them a chance. It does not confuse.

If you start this simple way, with letters and sounds, most children are ready by 4th birthday. It is only with the whole-word start that teachers think children are 'not ready', that learning to read takes years and years, and that children who are dyslexic develop problems. Phonics rescues dyslexics.

Phonics, intensive, systematic phonics-first, will schoolproof your child against the modern, fashionable infant teaching, and the National Curriculum.

Before you begin

Read each day's programme through before you start, the day before, to make sure you have all the materials you need. If you are worried about doing something wrong, or that will conflict with the teaching in the school, read pages 111 to 121 before you begin.

The first task is to learn 26 letters, how write each one, and its sound. This book gives you ideas and a programme, but use your own ideas, too. Throughout the whole programme, both you and the pupil should be enjoying yourselves. Pour out the praise endlessly.

If the pupil gets stuck or makes a mistake, avoid saying "No" or "That's wrong". See if any of it is right. Say, "Let's try again", "Have another look" or perhaps "Slow down". Later on, say, "You have got six letters right, in the right order, and now you need just one more letter to get it right. LISTEN to the word again...Now -- where have you lost a sound? Where would you need to add a letter in your spelling?" If it is "just one of those days", LAUGH and say, "Well, tomorrow is another day!"

Aim at about 30 minutes a day, but this is not rigid. Use your judgement. Some good days may allow an hour, other days ten minutes, but try to do a bit each day, even if it is only a game. Some American schools, with excellent results, spend up to 3 hours a day with 6-year-olds, by varying the activity -- handwriting, spelling, reading rules, story, Hangman etc.

Give the pupil as much time as he needs to puzzle out a word. For some children some steps may be slow. If you can see that there is a block, tell the word and go on, but telling the word is a last resort. We are trying to convince the pupil that he can read the words! Telling a word also may give the impression that reading must be fast. In the end it will be, but when you are learning HOW to read, give the learner time, no hurry,

Letters/sounds

The child will learn to write each letter by going over the large letters, from p.8 but you also need a large card, with the alphabet written in two lines in large, black letters. I also underline the vowels in red. You need 26 small cards about an inch (2 cms) square, with one letter written on each. I put the lower case on one side, and capitals on the other in a different colour. You will need extra small cards for commonly used letters: d f r s etc. --you will soon realise which they are.

The first step is giving the pupil one of the small cards and seeing if he can find that shape among other letters. If you feel finding one letter among 26 is too big a task, put 9 or 12 letters on a smaller, square card, and give the child one letter. If you give him a w, can he find the w among the 9 or 12 letters? If he can do this, and is talking, he is ready to start learning to read. If he is 3 and not talking, teaching him to read by this phonic method is a form of speech therapy and can help him to learn to talk at the same time. The sooner they start, the better. By school age, all children are ready, if you start with letters. It is trying to make them start with whole words that makes them appear to be "not ready".

I make a big card with two straight lines of letters:

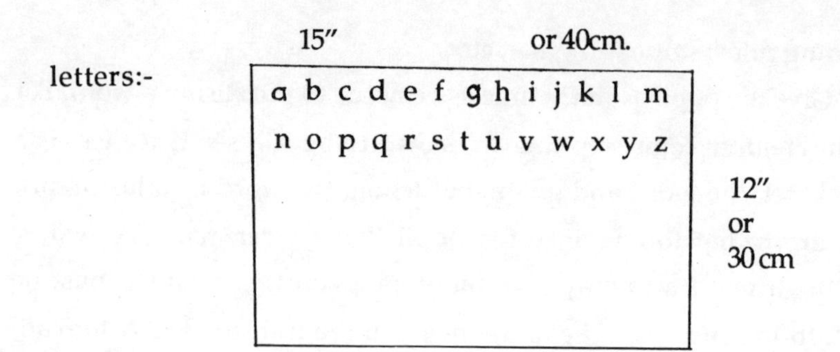

but some people prefer to arrange the letters in an arch like a rainbow, with a bottom-left, m at the top and z bottom-right.

At first you will give the child just one letter to match up by its shape, then as he gets better at this, you can give him all the 9 or 12 letters, to match onto the card. When he can do this easily, you can then let him match them up on the big alphabet-card. Seeing the 26 letters shows him that learning the letters is finite; he can see how many he has to learn altogether.

You can use these letters and the big card all through the programme. At some point, the child will learn the alphabet by singing it, but you will be surprised how quickly they learn the place for each letter. Using the small letters is a painless way to improve spelling. The child can pick out letters for sounds he can hear, and instead of red ink on mistakes, you just have to re-arrannge letters, or let him re-arrange them, or take out wrong letters, and leave a space for a missing letter. He then has to listen to the word and hear how the spoken word does not match the letters he has chosen, and to hear what letters he needs to provide the missing sounds.

WE READ WITH OUR EARS.

WE SPELL WITH OUR EARS.

At the same time that the pupil is learning that letters have sounds and shapes, that are written in a particular way, and how to hold a pencil, and that letters sit on lines,he is also going to learn the very valuable skill -- a trick, really -- of hearing sounds in words. On small cards the size of playing cards, write a 3-letter word on one side and stick or draw a picture on the other. Show the pupil the word, point to each letter and sound it, and make sure the child is LISTENING. It is a good idea to start with letters than can continue, like fffooooox, or Ssssaaaammm, so that you can continue the sounds without a break while you point to letters. For the first two or three, the child may not grasp what he is supposed to do, and you will have to show him that when you sound out fffoooox, there is a picture on the reverse, of a "fox". Then you can introduce words like cat where the c is a sharp sound, and extending it would be artificial like stuttering. This is the training in listening to sounds that helps, not listening to "environmental sounds" like beans or rice rattling in a tin.

Reading, writing and spelling are all learned at the same time.

Direction

When the child is going over the letters, in this book, or watching you point to letters on the 2-sided cards as you sound out, or writing words for himself, or playing the games, he is always going left-right. This prevents reversals of saw/was, no/on, etc. The left-right direction becomes automatic.

This programme is multi-sensory, that is to say that while the pupil is looking at the letter with his eyes, he will sound it with his voice and thus hear it with his ears, and write it or go over it with his finger using his muscles. This helps to prevent fidgeting, and helps concentration. By using all his senses (except smell and taste!) you never need to worry about his strengths and weaknesses.

The pupil will learn letters one at a time, and at the same time will write them, sound them out and learn to join them up into words, and to break words down into sounds which he can then spell. I do not teach a then b then c, d, e because this makes b and d very close together. I suggest you first teach the letters that start with the same action as c:

c a d g

and then o. Get d firmly fixed, starting with up-and-back round...,leave b nearly to the end, and this prevents b/d confusion. Leave q to the end , because there is no simple 3-letter word with a q.

How long will it all take?

This programme is set out as Day 1, Day 2, but this is only a guide. While some children will go through it much faster than others, older children will not need to spend much time on the letters Just make sure they do know 26, that they sound y as i and not yer. Adults may use this programme to brush up their spelling. But we do need to raise expectations.

Reading schemes go on for many years, but Gertrude Linnane says she teaches young children to read in 28 hours. At half an hour a day, that would be 56 days. An untrained American parent wrote a book called "Teach your child in 60 days". Other American teachers talk of teaching reading "in a couple of months". I mention these examples to contrast what happens in most schools now, to show you what can happen, but all children should learn to read, write and spell in two years or less.

Most children are ready by their 4th birthday, so should read by 6th birthday. For children older than 6, parents should not accept the advice, "Don't worry. He'll catch on."

6 MILLION DID NOT

Day 1

Put today's date__________

Sit at a table with your child. For convenience, I shall refer to the pupil as "he" and the teacher as "she", but pupils are boys and girls, and I have known some excellent father teachers.

You have probably already read a story to your child, and he knows that you can look at print and say words. We do not need to labour this. Use the head-lines of a newspaper to show that there are single letters — "This is a letter, and this, and this...—" and that they are grouped together in what we call words, with spaces in between so that you can see where one word ends and the next begins. We read letters and words from left to right, and line by line from top to bottom of the page. Does the child know what 'top' and'bottom' mean?

Teaching left-right direction, it is better to teach it as "We go this way", moving your finger, rather than using the words 'left' and 'right', unless your pupil already knows left and right for certain. In a classroom, you could put a Teddy up on the wall to the left of the blackboard and say, "We go from Teddy, this way," or fix a picture of something, with a paperclip, to the page, and say, "We start at this side, and go this way..." showing by your action, and holding the child's hand as he points, to move it from left to right to get the feel of the direction.

Now, start with <u>cat</u>, on the next page.

Make sure the pencil grip is correct, the <u>first</u> time the child holds a crayon or pencil. The thumb and side of the long finger do the gripping, with the index finger sitting loosely on top. Prevent bad habits. If pencil grip is a problem, you can get a good, cheap (about 25p) plastic, triangular pencil grip from E. J. Arnold of Leeds or Taskmaster of Leicester.

Explain how the symbols in the letters in 'cat' work: you put the point of the pencil inside the black circle, and go the way the arrow points (explain arrow), along the dots, and there-and-back along the dashes. If there is only one arrow, the whole letter is completed before lifting the pencil up from the page, as in c and a, but t has two starts. Always give the child a line to write on — two if you wish, as I do in this book, see later. When two lines are used, tall letters go above the top line, and tails below the bottom line.

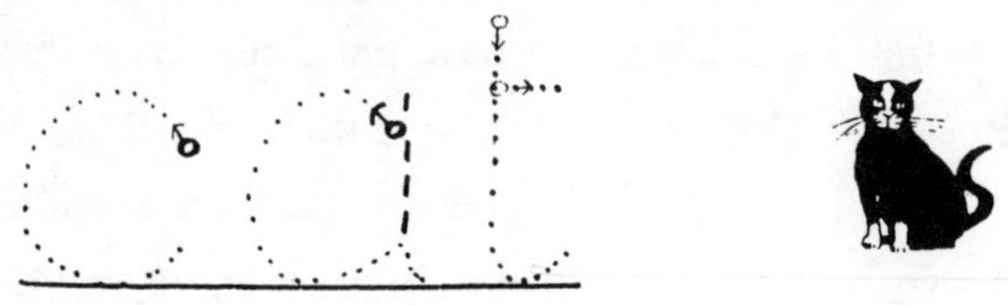

You will see that the picture of the cat is black and white, and is NOT part of some fascinating story. The fascination is in learning to make letters talk. The picture is only there in case the child forgets the three letters, and can then remind himself from the picture, and not by asking teacher. Children must ask what they do not understand, but we want to make them as independent as we can, from the start.

Let the pupil go over each letter many times, with his finger, with a pale-coloured felt pen or crayon, then darker pen. Let him practise on scrap paper. He must go over a letter, look at it, sound it, hear it, all at the same time. He must learn the sound of c as in cat. If you wish him to learn "Cee says k", the name and the sound, you can. In the end he will have to know both name and sound, but at the beginning the sounds are essential.

To emphasise just where you start a c, NOT at the top, you can use, or draw, a clock, and show that c starts not at the top at 12 o'clock, but at 2, and goes back up, right round 3/4 of a circle, ending at 4. The a starts with a c but keeps going. Let the pupil go over the letters until he knows them, writing and sounding.

He must also hear that c-a-t makes cat; he must be able to hear the bits and join them, and hear that cat starts with the c sound, then a then t. This work lends itself to class teaching. You can set out the alphabet on the big card, pick out the three letters to make the word cat and then show how you put the letters back in their place. You can do this for all the letters as they are learned.

Use the cards described on page 5, with a word on one side and picture on the reverse, asking "What is the picture on the back? It is a p....i....n." and the child will say "Pin", turn the card over and the child will see that he has got it right. Using these cards, you can use letters before the child learns them — you sound out the letters one at a time, then as he learns letters, he can sound out the ones he knows. Let him see you are sounding out letters one at a time. If you have cards for: pan, pen, pin, he will realise that each letter matters, that we cannot read just from 1st letter, or even first-and-last letter. All the letters matter. You can have log, leg, jug, mug, rug; mat man men map; cup cap tap cat cot; bat bag; bin tin lips; fox box; and then a few with 3 sounds but 4 letters: bell, doll; sock neck; kiss.

I do not use 'bed' very often, because it mirrors almost perfectly. That is why I do not use it to teach how to differentiate b and d.

Games

There are at every stage three games: Pairs, bingo and a board game like snakes and ladders (see page 12). You can play the games from the start, sounding out letters not yet taught, so that as more letters are learned, you give less and less help.

Pairs: For this, you need 52 playing cards, blank one side. You can get blank visiting cards from your local printer for about 1p each, or you can buy 1000 playing cards, either blank one side or blank both side, from E. J. Arnold, Leeds for £16 (1990 price). On 13 cards you write a 3-letter word in one colour (cap cat pan pen pin rug jug cup log man men bin bat, for instance), and the same 13 words in a contrasting colour on another 13 cards. If you are sticking pictures (not drawing), choose words you can find pictured in, e.g. a mail order catalogue, the right size and uncomplicated. Make a set of 13 pictures, twice, giving 52 cards in all. There are at least three ways you can use these cards.

1) Make a pile of all the word cards face-up, and round them spread the 26 pictures face-up. Sound out the 3 letters on each card, have the pupil say the complete word and find the picture, until the table is clear. I call this "Clear the table". If you record starting and finishing times (min/sec.), and work out how long it took, and put this down with the date, he can play against the clock, trying to beat his own time the next day. Only do this (timing) if it is fun, and not if it upsets. Only do this once a day.

2) Pairs (Pelmanism) Put all cards out face-down. A player turns up one card, then a second: if they are a pair, either two words or two pictures, or word and picture, that is a pair, and the player has another turn, until he makes a mistake. If 52 cards over-faces the pupil, start with only half the cards, but be sure you play with full sets of 4 cards for each word.

3 Old Maid. Remove one card face down , not seen. Deal all the remaining cards among the players, who sort out their cards by removing all the pairs. This leaves 6 or 8 cards per player. Next, each player puts down a card, face down, then they all move their card to the player on their left, and pick up the card from the right. This card may make another pair, which is discarded. The one who is left with the odd card is the Old Maid.

Use your own judgement how long to go on, each day.

SNAP is much too fast a game to play at this stage.

Day 2

Go over the three letters in "cat" as before. Begin to sing the alphabet, using the names ay-bee-see. Point to each letter (on the big card) as you sing. As each letter is learned, have the pupil "draw" the letter in the air as big as possible, swinging the arm from the shoulder with large arm movements, again saying the sound as he swings his arm. This is excellent in class-work as it enables a teacher to spot at once any child making the wrong movement.

Play the DICE GAME. This is a board game like snakes-and-ladders. Making these can be a happy family activity, cutting out the pictures, drawing ladders and a slide. Remember you can only use simple three-letter words, not saw, car, eye, where there is not one simple sound per letter. You cannot put "Have another turn" until you have taught th, er, ur. I make the first letter in any square a capital (see pages 12-13). I teach capitals as they crop up. For the 3-letter stage, the instructions can be "Run on to a man", "Run on to a red six". The first square after Start I usually make "Run on six" to turn a slow start into a good start. I explain that letters do not always make their simple sound, that to does not sound like the beginning of top, and that Go is not the beginning of got but the o says its name: Go. I say that sometimes vowels can say their name (no, go so) and that with "Go back..." if you have a sound twice, doll bell, kiss pass, or back neck lock (ck) you only say it once. This answers the question that may arise in their mind, but we do not need to give this much practice at this stage. We are only learning letters today.

Use the card with pictures on one side, word on the other, sound out, and provide practice in listening to sounds to make them into words.

Win!			Go back to a dog
Run on to a jug			Run to a bat
		Run on to a cot	Run on to a cat
Start	Run on six	Run on to a box	Run to a pan

Run on to a man

Run on to a zip

on

Run on up to a dog

on

Go up

Run on up to a leg

Day 3

Go over the three letters in cat. See if your pupil can sound them out one at a time, random, not just in the order of c-a-t.

Play the dice game, and Pairs.

Show the child his own name. Perhaps let him watch you write it in large letters, in yellow felt-pen or highlight, then let him go over it, sounding it where possible.

Day 4

Learn the letter o (see below), then show how from the four letters c,a,t,o we can also make cot, act.

If "act" is a new word, explain it. Look again at the irregular word to so that the pupil can see the t and hear it work. Say "It looks like to (the beginning of top) and we say too" making the oo short.

Day 5, 6

Learn the letters d, g and write the word, see next page. Write the three letters, large, in the air, saying the sound.

Set out the large alphabet card and put the six letters (on small cards) on top of the alphabet-letters, in their place, so the pupil can see he has had six letters.

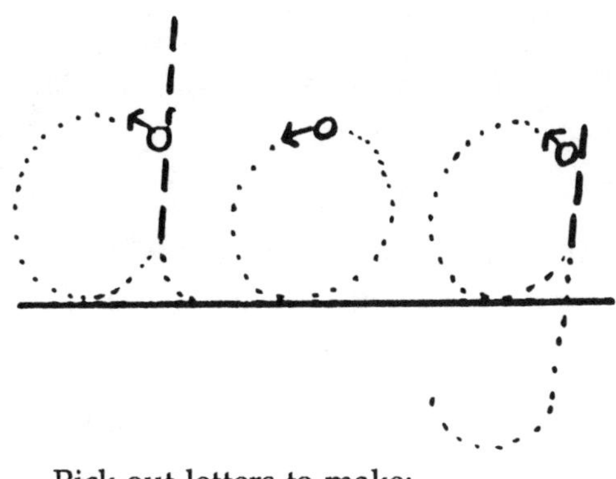

Pick out letters to make:

tag cog cod dot got god

Explain new words like cog (cad, if you wish to use it). Learning to read includes spelling, and increasing vocabulary, meaning, comprehension. Show that knowing only 6 letters we can read 11 words.

Play the games, leaving the pupil to sound out the six letters he has had, while you sound out the other 20, but let him say each complete word while looking at it. Let him take his time. Always let him take as much time as he needs. Speed has no virtue at this stage.

Day 7, 8

Learn the letters f, x.

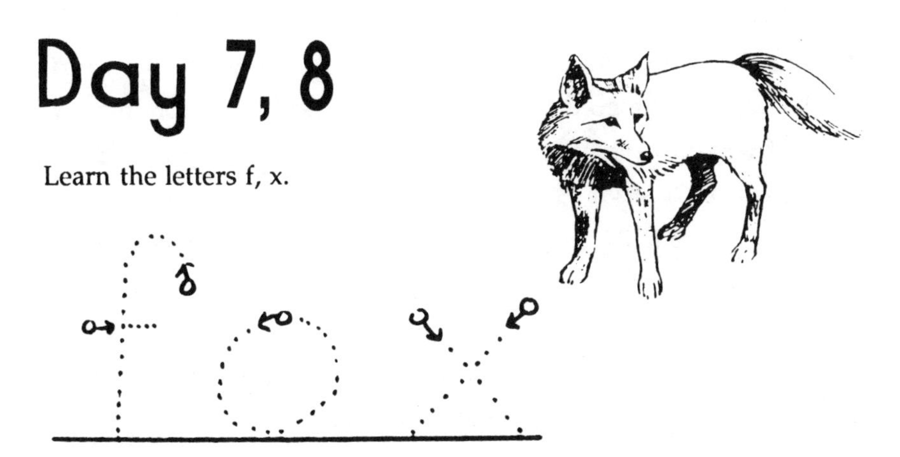

f begins with the top of a circle.

Set out the alphabet with 8 letters, and show how we can build up earlier words, plus:

fat fad fog cox (the one who calls the stroke in the Boat Race)

Make sure the action for f is up-and-over-and-down. It is not down-up like an r.

x: Children sometimes find it difficult to make the parts of an x, z and k slope down properly. If so, draw a square box and show how you can fit the x (and z and k) into it. For the x and z the down-slope goes from one top corner to the opposite bottom one:

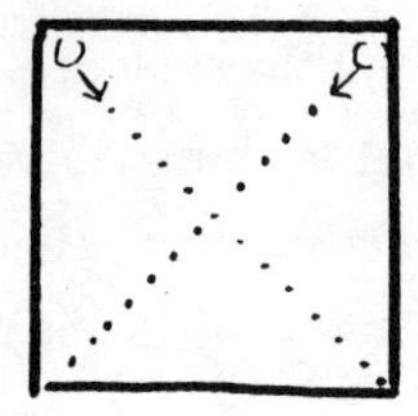

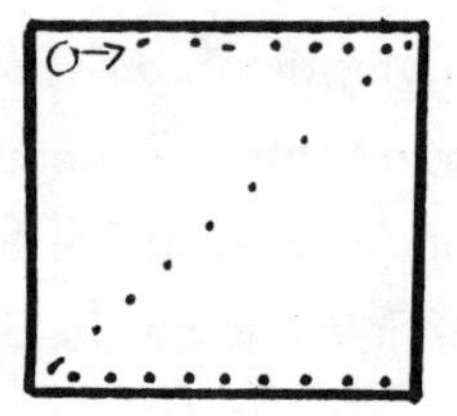

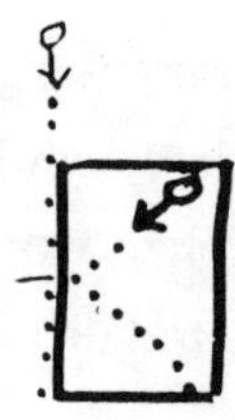

Play the dice game and pairs, sounding out all but the 8 letters taught. If the pupil forgets what a letter says, show him the word he did, and let him go through it to find the letter and work out for himself what it says. If the letter he wants is at the end of 'dog', then it says the last sound in 'dog'.

If you teach children a for apple, b for ball, you can end up with them thinking 'a says apple', and giving too much importance to the first letter. This is why I use only a few words in which they can learn the letters, and they are getting left-right direction and hearing-sounds-in-words all the time, non-stop.

Clear speech helps spelling. f is said by biting the bottom lip. This must be clearly fixed to the letter f, so that when th is introduced, it is NOT f.

x is the only letter that makes two sounds: ks. Say other words like

box fox fix mix six next exact expand

and explain them if necessary, so that the pupil can hear the x sounds.

Day 9, 10

Set out the alphabet, and put out the 8 small letter-cards. Revise their sound.

Play pairs.

Learn v and n in:

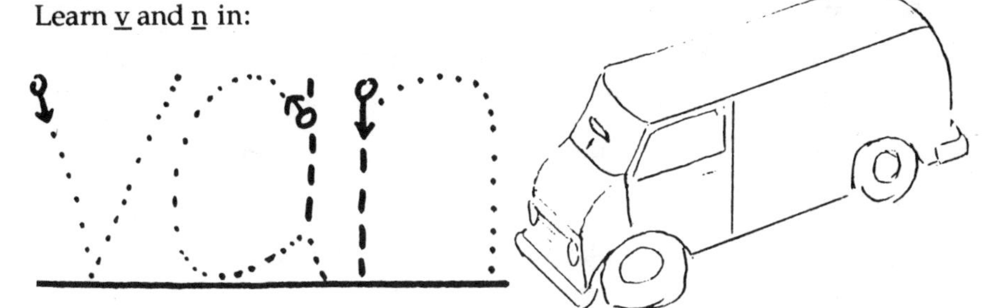

V is the shape of a valley.

Explain what valleys are, find a picture of one. We go up a mountain and down the other side, and the point is at the top. Between two mountains you go down to the river at the bottom, down into a valley, and up the next mountain. A valley is, in a way, the opposite of a mountain, and it has the point at the bottom. The point should be a point, and not a curve. The v is made of two straight lines, down-up.

Show how knowing two more letters gives access to more words:

can nan nag not tan and

Let the child build up those words by picking out the right letters as you say each word, and then replacing them.

Day 11, 12, 13

Learn the letters z, i, p.

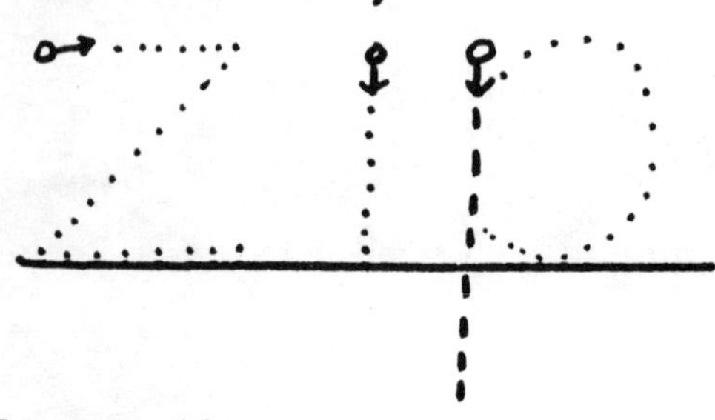

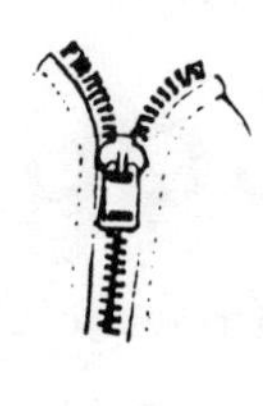

For z see p.16

Draw the i with the downstroke first and then the dot. Draw the p as "down-up-and-round" with the bubble sitting on the line.

Add the three letters to the alphabet, and let the child make up new words, by listening sounds:

tip   dig   fig   pig   cap   pod (pea-pod)   pat

pot   top   fit   pit

Play pairs and the board game, letting the pupil sound out more and more letters each day.

Day 14, 15

Learn the letters w and e.

A w is rather like two v's and the French call it double-v! You can see lots of w on the pavement, where the lid of the water-stop-cock

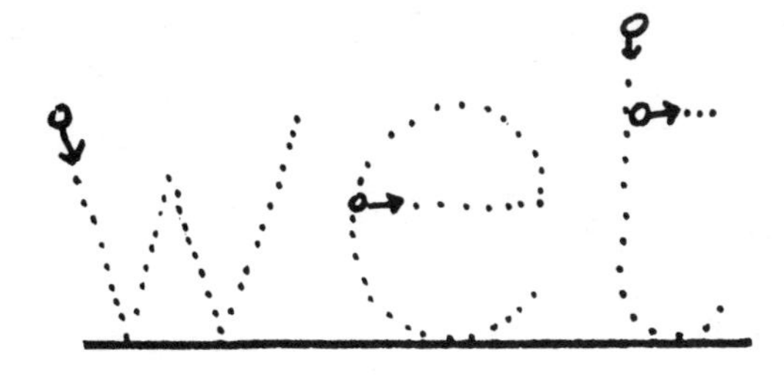

is marked "water". Set out the alphabet card, and add w and e, making 14 letters —past half-way.

Make new words:

net vet get pet den ten

Play the games.

———

You have now been working for two weeks. The rate set out is about a letter a day. Young children with plenty of time are in no rush and you can take more time. Use and trust your own judgement. Older children and adults may go through all 26 letters in 10 minutes, but it is worthwhile to check that they really do know 26 and not 25! and how to write each one.

You will by now see that all the interest lies in making the letters talk. We are not looking at pictures, discussing a story, predicting what happens next. We are learning to read and spell, how to hear sounds and join them up into a spoken word, and break it down into first, middle and last sound and thus spell it, and how to write. We are making the left-right habit rock-hard, and we are building confidence, showing the child that he does not need us to read the words for him, because <u>he</u> can. (This is the opposite of paired reading, apprenticeship, etc.)

Day 16

Learn the letter r.

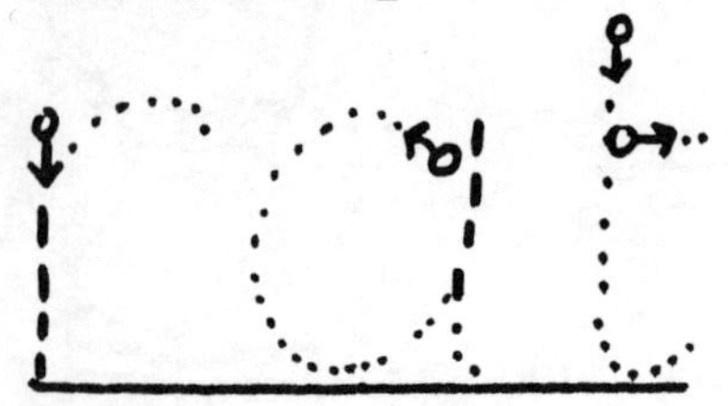

Show how r has the same movement as n at the beginning, but stops short.

Make words: rip rod rid ran rot

Play games.

Day 17

Learn the letter m.

Show how m, n and r all start the same, down-up.

Sound m with the lips closed, humming, not "mer".

Make new words:

mat ram dam dim mop map

Play games.

Day 18

Learn the letter u.

Sound its sound (not name) and say:

U goes under and up
(short sound as in gun.)

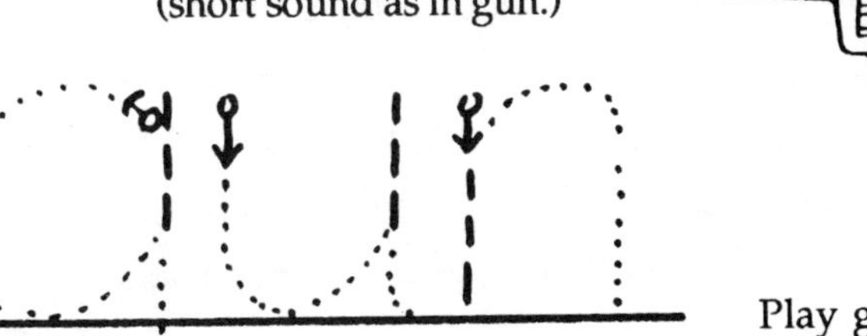

Play games.
Make new words:

rug mug cup but puff dug up

Present the words bull, pull, put, and say that u has two sounds. Usually it says the sound in gun, but it can sound like the two oo in hook, in bull, pull, put, and for this sound the lips are forward. If the first sound (as in gun) does not make a word, when sounding out, try the second sound.

— — — — —

You have now gone through all five vowels. Pick them out. Did you underline them in red? Show them, and say, "Their names are a y, ee, I, oh, you". So far we are sounding their short sound as in:

pat pet pit pot put.

Some programmes train the pupil to put any consonant in front of these vowels, and say the joint sound:

ba be bi bo bu; ma me mi mo mu and so on.

Others do the reverse, putting the vowel first:

at et it ot ut

These are not usually words, but are practice in joining sounds. You can do this if you wish. I keep to sounding out real words.

Day 19

Learn the letter l — a long line.

Make new words:

let lit lot lap log lag leg lad pull doll bull

Pronunciation. The l at the end should be the same as the l at the beginning. In words like bell, tell, apple, the l should NOT say oo. Apple is NOT appoo. The tongue should be up behind the top teeth, and the lips should not come forward. If the pupil is saying we-oo for well, use a mirror and let him see that he is not saying a l. Let the pupil reach high into the air and then come down to draw an l, - l: long line. Play games.

Day 20 - 22

Learn the letters that start with an l: h k b

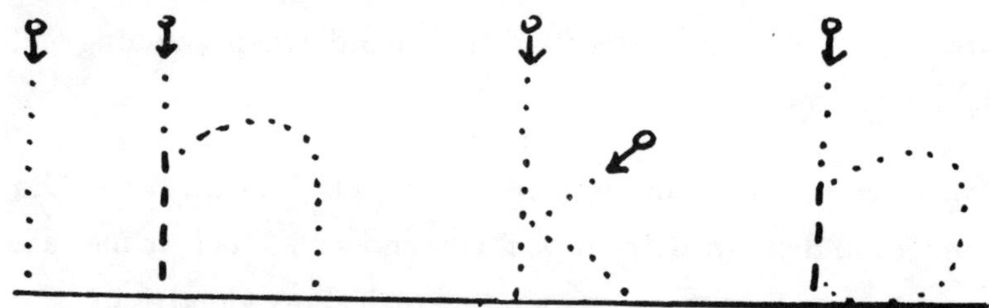

When k is at the end of a short word (one syllable), we must put a c in front of it:

pack	peck	pick	lock	duck	
rack	deck	tick	rock	stuck	
back	neck	lick	mock	buck (bucking bronco)	
hack			dock		and slang for dollar.
				puck	(used in ice hockey)

Learn b (a bat and a ball)

For older children who have confused b/d, you show that they are NOT the same. Only one starts at the top —a b. You draw a straight line down (a bat) and on the right of it you draw the ball, so that the bat can hit the ball along the empty line (to write) or along the line the way we read (to read). The child must think: bat and ball for a b.

d is different. It starts with a c and it is the only letter where we draw up to the tall part and do not start with a down movement. I ask if the child knows a-b-c-d. If he does, I show him how to tap out the a-b with his non-writing hand, and then draw the c and keep going to make a d; to get d right, he must say to himself, a-b-C-d.

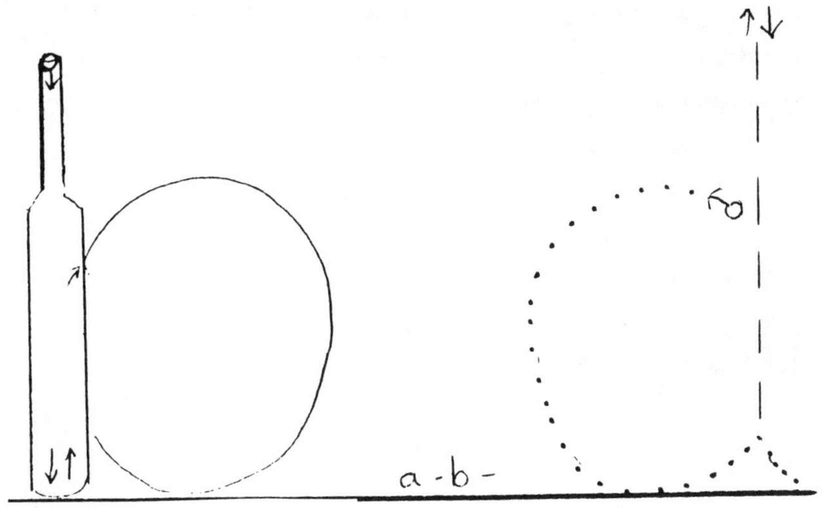

Day 23

Learn the letter s. It fits inside a circle.

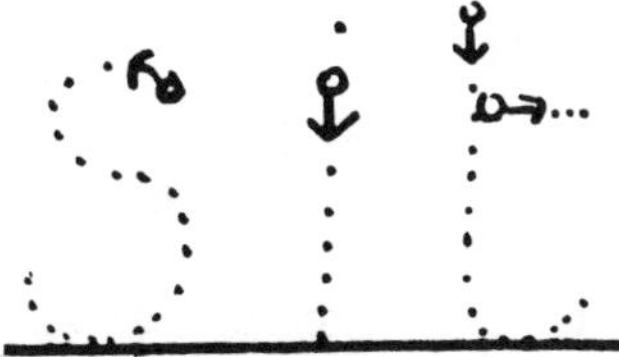

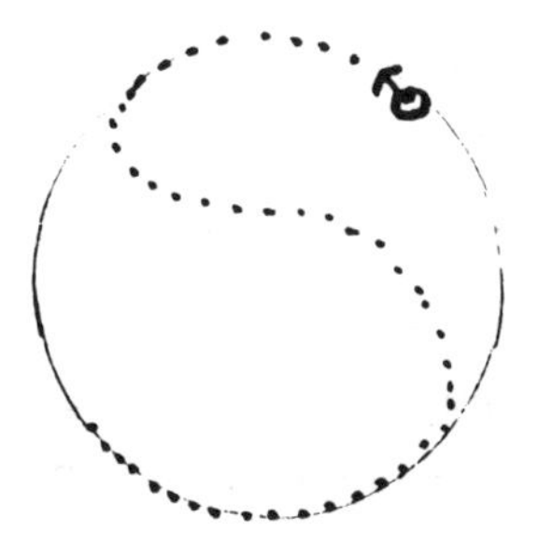

The top bend of the s should be, if anything, smaller, tighter, than the bottom.

We can say that s is the shape of a snake and it makes the same sound. Do snakes hiss? I have never heard one!

Make new words:

sat set sun sip sad sag sum gas

sick sock suck

Say words in singular and plural: hat, hats

pig, pigs

dog, dogs

and encourage the pupil to hear that by putting an s at the end, we have the word that means more than one of whatever it is

one dog, ten dogs.

Choose some doing words (verbs) and do the same:

run, runs hit, hits dig, digs

and explain that we say: I run,you run, but he runs

I dig, you dig, but he digs

Show where and why we use an s in these ways.

Day 24

Learn the letter j.

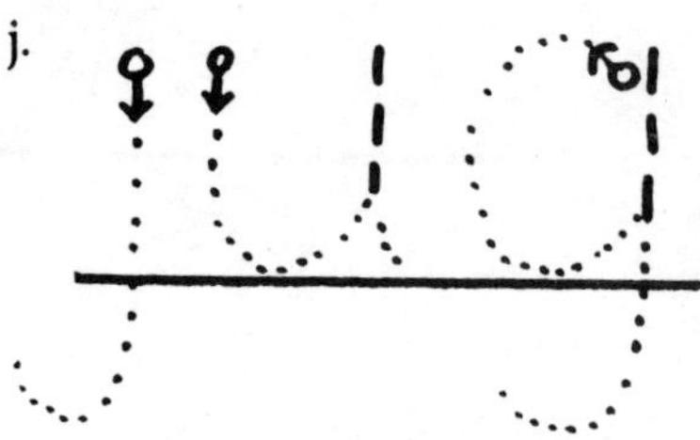

Make new words: jet Jack jot jam

Show that Jack has a different kind of j, a capital J, and that it has a line across the top instead of a dot.

Explain that we call all the big letters capitals, and we use them at the beginning of names of people, towns, countries, rivers, days, months, and at the beginning of a sentence. We use "sentences" when we say something, like "I am hungry" or "It is raining". Letters make words, words make sentences, sentences make stories.

Sing the alphabet. Touch each letter as you sing it. We still have to learn q and y.

Day 25

Y can make two sounds, the long sound in fly, cry, and the short sound in happy, system. If you put that short sound in front of -ellow (like a short i), the final sounded word is yellow as we normally say it. You can do the same with yes, yesterday, yacht. If you do this, it means that we only have two sounds to learn for y. Making a y say 'yer' is not a good idea, because we do not say"happ-yer" etc. and while hardly any words begin with a y, hundreds of words have it in the middle and at the end.

At this beginning stage, let y just say the short sound. Therefore we have to move on to words with four sounds: D-a-dd-y

If you are teaching a class, you may be able to find names ending in y among your pupils: Harry, Henry, Polly, Billy, Sandy, Betty, Jenny, Patsy.

You can point out that often the consonant before a short y is double: daddy, happy, funny, hurry, pussy, Teddy.

Point out that five of the letters are underlined in red, and say "These are vowels." Y works like a vowel and can change places with an i — "Change the y into i and add es". The other 20 letters are called consonants.

Day 26

This is the Big Day — the very last letter, so make a big fuss!

In English words, the letter q is always followed by a u, and the two letters together say kw.

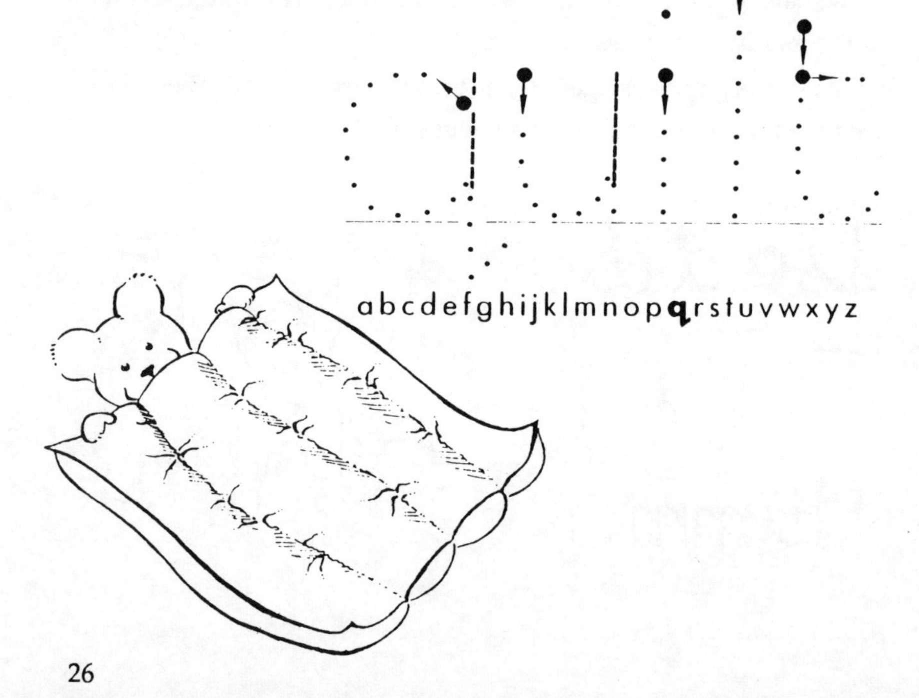

Make the word quiz

quick— remind that the k sound has 2 letters.

Now you are ready for two new tools of learning, a Bingo game, and a booklet, "Is it?" You can make them.

For each Bingo game, I use 32 words, 16 on each card size 5" x 6" (13 cm x 15 cm), and each word on 32 separate small cards. If only two play, they can use the words to "cover up", but if more than 2 play, each player needs the larger card and also 16 small, blank cover-up cards. I cut these from an old tissue box.

Each player reads out one word from the pile, and the player who has that word on his card takes the small card to cover up that word on his card. I turn them over, so that as play proceeds, words disappear and you can only see the words you still need. When a player has a line, he shouts"Bingo!" and gets a small prize (peanut, raisin, Smartie). A line can be either horizontal (across), vertical (down) or diagonal (corner to corner) — and use these long words! Expand vocabulary all the time. I usually play five wins per card: Line, line, line, "round the outside" 12 squares, and Full Card. (See next page)

"Is it?"

From now on, you can make "Is it?" books for each stage. Take a dozen or so sheets of paper. Cut an A4 into 4 quarters; this is a suitable size. Write a 3-letter word on one side and stick or draw a picture matching that word on the other side. Fasten them together into a booklet, words first. The pupil cannot see word and picture at the same time. All my materials are devised to fight the bad habit of guessing. The idea is NOT to learn words, so nowhere in my programme should a child "learn words" as wholes, like flashcards.

The child sounds out and reads the word, and then turns over the page to see if he has got it right. He can do this 3-4 times, right through the book, and then he is ready to try spelling, starting at

sun	men	tap	cat
red	get	gun	rod
lot	dog	man	rag
wax	hit	set	fix

The other 16 words I use are:

Bingo.

ran	wet	sit	hot	run
van	let	wig	fox	jug
bag	ten	zip		cup
		win		
		lid		

(Total 32 words)

the back of the booklet. He can see the picture this time, tries to spell it, then turns back to see if he has got the spelling right.

The aim is to keep the child doing the same thing, sounding out 3-letter words, but to provide variety by presenting the activity under as many different guises as possible. For instance, the pink "Now I can spell" workbook by Ridout (Collins pub.) fits nicely into this stage of the work.

It is a good thing if we can keep spelling up to the reading. I tell children they read with their ears, and even more, they spell with their ears. On page 30 are five columns, one for each vowel. Say a word to the child, and ask him to listen for the vowel in the middle. Which is the middle vowel? He can then find the correct column and try to spell that word. You can use words from the Bingo, the dice game, and the Ridout book, any words that have 3-letters, 3 sounds and not words like <u>fur</u> where the <u>ur</u> makes one sound, or <u>was</u> where the <u>wa</u> does not make the sound in wax. Where possible, let the pupil do his own checking.

The aim is plenty of practice so that the response to a 3-letter word is automatic and fast, but NOT from flash-card work.

Truly graded reading books at this stage are rare. Primary Phonics makes them, 10 books in set 1 (Titles: Mac and Tab, The Tin Man, A1, The Jet, Ben Bug Ed and so on) from Educators Publishing Service Inc., 75 Moulton St., Cambridge, Mass. 02138.

Writing

If the child is pressing on too hard, in writing, turn the page over and let him feel the ridges he has made. Tell him pressing on will make him tired. Buy a cheap (20p) propelling pencil with a thin lead, so that it breaks when he presses too hard.

Letters

Set out the loose alphabet on the big alphabet card, and have the child pick out the 3 letters needed for a word, arrange them correctly, say the word and then put the letters back in their place. Sing the alphabet.

It sounds silly to say that if a child learns quickly, he will learn more quickly! but if too much time elapses (3-4 days) between one lesson and the next, the learning fades. But beyond that, if a child learns quickly, he is aware of his progress and that is an incentive. If the learning is slow, the child is not aware of it, and he feels he is

a	e	i	o	u
wet		dog		

just plodding on without getting anywhere. An hour a day for 10 days gives more progress than the same 10 hours spread over 20 days.

Day 27-30

"Day 27" is not hard and fast. This programme merely sets out one version of teaching phonics, and a good phonic programme will not vary too far from it. We have had so much of "All children are different" without the other half of the truth "All children have common needs," we have had "Don't worry; he'll catch on" and "Reading to your child is the best help", so that many parents and teachers now either do not know how to set about teaching letters, etc., or are afraid to do so.

This programme is SAFE, safe for all ages including adults, safe for pre-schoolers, dyslexics, gipsies, people in prison, everyone. Just use your common sense as to how long to take over each step. All I provide is a bit of an idea how long it should take, but learning to read should not take more than two years for ANYBODY except the very, very severely dyslexic, who need to attend a residential school such as that run by Martin Phillips (Old Brettenham, Suffolk). Such people are about .3% (point three per cent) of the population.

When a child can read 3-letter words, work with 4-letter words, but again only words that have 4 sounds, i.e. not ship where the sh is one sound, not rake where the e is silent. In schools that can do classwork and other work, and with variety can easily spend 1 $^1/_2$ to 3 hours a day on reading and spelling, three days may be enough time for the 4-letter stage.

Make a dice-game, bingo, pack of cards for Pairs, and an "Is it?" book. The pupil can work some pages of the "Now I can spell" Red and Orange books but these are not really graded, so many of the

a	e	i	o	u
			stop	

pages will have to wait until later in the programme.

Many teachers and some schemes spend time working on what they call "blends", st, sp tr, or "letter-strings" like str, spl. I believe that if a child really grasps how to read 3- and 4-letter words, and knows s and t, we do not need to give any extra time to learning st. ST is just two ordinary letters one after the other. Why make it seem difficult, why provide something extra to learn when we do not need it?

When we come, soon, to what I call letter-groups, where two letters must be read together to make one sound, like sh,then is the time to have the child notice two letters together, but when reading vest, flat, flag, it is enough to go through the sequence of letters, sound them out and L I S T E N

The words I use for 4-letter bingo are:

camp	rest	drip	pink	cost	lump
fast	send	fist	ring	drop	must
flag	sent	lick	spin	lock	jump
hand	vest	limp	wind	song	just
rang	went	list	wing	stop	
sack		wink			
sand					

Day 31-35

This is the last stage of reading with just single letters. You move on to words of any length: stamp, crust, comic, with 5 letters, on to: clinic, hospital, caravan, interesting, Japan, America, Canada... Use your atlas. If you do not have one, Philips' Modern School Atlas is suitable. Many countries and towns have simply spelled names, and we must keep our child's mind expanding! Try Scotland, Finland, India, Iran, Mexico, Italy, Brazil; and states in America: Florida, Mississippi, Texas, Indiana; and Atlantic.

Vowels in some words do not give a clear sound, We say bask i t. sev'n. It is a good idea to say the word as it is spelt, basKETT, sevEN, making the e say the sound in "ten", for the first 2-3 times we say any word. Say:

hos-pi-tal, (as in cat)
probl e m (as in ten)

Some people need extra practice in listening to, and hearing, sounds in words. Now and then practise saying words as follows:

CRUST	c - rust
	cr - ust
	cru - st
	crus - t

The leader (teacher) begins the word and the pupil completes it as two chunks, beginning and what is left, not as 5 separate sounds. Then, later on, practise breaking words up into sounds:

church	ch ur ch
cloud	c l ou d
paint	p ai n t
play	p l ay

Make a pairs game, a dice game, and Is it? book, and you can now make three bingo games.

Word bingo

stamp	stand	swank	basket	Frank	cramp
nasty	flask	grasp	plant	rabbit	rascal
plank	seven	eleven	expand	empty	lemon
sting	bring	index	swing	drink	comic
along	problem	trumpet	bullet	hundred	rusty
crust	stump				

Remember: If you have a sound twice, either a double letter or ck, you only say it once.

Girls' names bingo

Anne	Betty	Molly	Linda	Peggy	Polly
Amanda	Brenda	Camilla	Glenda	Matilda	Emma
Olga	Pamela	Edna	Elsa	Veronica	Joanna
Lydia	Stella	Vanessa	Hilda	Sally	Pat
Rebecca	Kim	Sylvia	Dolly	Hannah	Jessica
Mildred	Winifred				

Choose column of first sounded vowel.

a	e	i	o	u

Boys' names bingo

Alan	Bill	Alec	Brendan	Eric	Harry
Henry	Frank	Fred	Adam	Kit	Ronald
Rex	Sam	Robin	Tom	Colin	Derek
Duncan	Kim	Kevin	Tim	Jim	Max
William	Winston	Trevor	Angus	Ross	Cliff
Jack	Patrick				

Spell words and girls' and boys' names in the columns on page 35. Put each word in the column of the first sounded vowel.

Bedtime stories

You can always read stoies to children for their pleasure. Now you can start letting the child read, puzzle out, the words you know he can read, the words with no letter-groups. As he learns more groups he will read more of the words, until he can take over.
BUT if he starts guessing or predicting, discourage this or stop books. Often victims of "real books" etc. will do quite well on this programme, not guessing on the games, but as soon as you give them a book they go back to guessing. This is a real barrier to progress.

Nagging is a misery. I put out 5 Smarties, and each time the child guesses, one Smartie goes back in the jar. I do not say a word. The pupils, sadly, think that guessing — fast — is better than getting it right at their own speed. Guessing is a terrible thing.

Day 36, 37

We do not need to wait until the child can "read off" (like a sight vocabulary) all the words .Right to the end of the programme and for the rest of his life, he will be coming to new words in which simple letters will say their sound; even in "rough" the r sounds simply. Being able to sound out and read words of any length, one letter one sound, is the first third of learning to read. The second third is learning the sounds for which there is not a letter, and for which we use 2 or more letters. The final third is fluency, which grows of its own accord.

As we learn new letter-groups, each one will give access to lots of new words, and we shall all the time keep coming to words and spelling patterns that we have already had.

Explain that while our alphabet has 26 letters, in speech we use 44 sounds, that is, we have more sounds than letters. This problem is solved by using 2 or more letters together to make extra sounds. It is really very clever and quite interesting, how letters work. (There are more ways than one to spell some sounds, but leave that for the moment. Do not complicate.)

The first two new sounds are oo and ee, Say: "One o says o (as in top) but two o's say oo "as in moon". Have the child repeat three times, "Two o's say oo" and then show him the next page. Here, and in later pages, are the only materials I use where the pupil can see word and picture together, and they are there to give the child independence. If he forgets what oo says, he can go back to that page and work it out, m...OO...n, the sound after m is the sound oo. Have him read the first four words, then explain that sometimes the oo, although the same sound, is shorter, as in book, cook, and have him read those words.

The ee is simpler. "Two e's say eeeee". Have him repeat this 3 times. If he forgets, have him repeat it 3 more times, then have him read the words in the list — which are NOT words to be "learned", not to form a sight vocabulary, NOT to be flashcarded or processed as whole words. A word is a letter-sequence, a sound-sequence.

Sing the alphabet. Play the games made previously.

Joined writing

You will see that I have joined together the letters that must be said together. Your pupil may do the same, as an introduction to joined writing. Please yourself

oo ee

moon tree

moon
cool
soon
room
look
cook
book
hook
good

tree
feel
heel
week
seem
green
see
bee

Remind that h is the blowy-letter. When you use it with another letter, you still blow — as in sh ch th.

We first learn sh, the sound we make to tell people to hush. Have the pupil say "sh", with his hand in front of his mouth, so that he can feel the wind of the blow.

Have him say three times,

"s...h says sh

(ess-aitch says sh)

Have him read the words listed, twice through.

Play the games from the previous sections.

Sing the alphabet.

Write a joined sh on scrap paper, in large letters with a yellow felt pen, or highlight, and let the child go over them, to get the feel of how you join letters.

Draw the letters separately and then add the joining bit in a different colour, to show the extra line. If you wish, he can go over the list of words, in felt pen.

Now that we are talking about letters, it is time to learn their names (as above, ess-aitch).

Day 38

sh

fish

fi sh
di sh
fla sh
cra sh
bru sh

sh o p
sh i p
sh o t
sh u t
shrimp

Day 39

ch

Read the words from the sh list
Remind that h is a blowy letter. With c it says a sound like a sneeze. Sh goes on longer, ch stops short.

Have the child (or class) repeat 3 times "C-h says ch".

Show that the picture is of a chin, and have the child find the ch in that word. Go through the list of ch words, with the pupil reading them,. Point out that such much rich just end with 'ch' but all the other words with a short vowel are spelt: t-ch:

p	atch
f	etch
h	itch
Sc	otch
h	utch

Sing the alphabet.

Play the previous games.

Write a large ch in a pale colour, joined, and have your pupil go over it, to learn the way to join.

chin

chin
chips
chop
chap

much
such
rich
crunch
fetch
ditch
match
scratch

Good speech helps good spelling. Remind that th is another letter-group with an h so there will be a blow in it.

In th the t stands for tongue, so have the child put the tip of his tongue out, and then blow, to make the sound of th.

Go back over a few pairs of letters, t/d, p/b, k/g, and have the child put his hand on his throat, to feel that with the first of a pair there is no tremble, but when we say d, b, g (in go), our throat vibrates (and they learn what "vibrate" means) because they are voiced. The t must be t, not ter, for this to work.

Today's letter-group can be both voiced (with tremble) and unvoiced. Have the child say the first words with unvoiced th, then voiced in this, then, that.

The child will sound out bath but when he realises its meaning, may change it to "baff". This needs very clear explaining, that there is no such word as baff, that for th we must put out the tip of tongue, but for f we bit our bottom lip.

Have the child say clearly:

deaf (cannot hear) and death;

Day 40

th

ba**th**

bath

path

with

think

this

that

then

them

the

three (3) and free (we did not have to pay for it. For a class, have the whole class say these words very distinctly, and for the next fortnight check the the th is properly pronounced. Against the influence of "Minder", "East Enders" etc., you will have to battle very hard. Can we rid our language of this wrong speech in this generation?

Marva Collins is a splendid teacher who aims for the stars, in a ghetto school in Chicago. She is a black lady teaching mostly black children but says, "I'm opposed to teaching black English because it separates black children from the rest of society; it also implies that they are too inferior to learn standard English usage." Read her book, "Marva Collins' Way" (ISBN 0-874-77310-5). How different from the depressing National Curriculum, which says "Do not teach Standard English too early"! We should give them Standard English from the start. We must start equalising up, not down.

We have now had oo, ee sh ch th, and it is time to make more games, Pairs, Bingo, dice game and "Is it?" book, using all five letter-groups. I only suggest Bingo words to save you the trouble of thinking them up:

been	chips	chop	chunk	cheek	feed
fetch	fish	food	good	green	hood
look	much	pool	sheep	shop	sweet
shot	shut	ship	seem	spoon	teeth
tooth	sheets	tree	think	this	thick
that	week				

You can dictate them a word at a time, and have the child choose the column on page 43 that has the first letter-group in it (teeth would go in ee. It can go in the th as well, if you wish.) This is practice in hand-writing. Remind the pupil not to press on too hard Check on his pencil-grip.

Now that we have done the word "the", the pupil can write about "Teddy on the Sands", page 44 on.

oo	ee	sh	th	ch

You can write about Teddy!

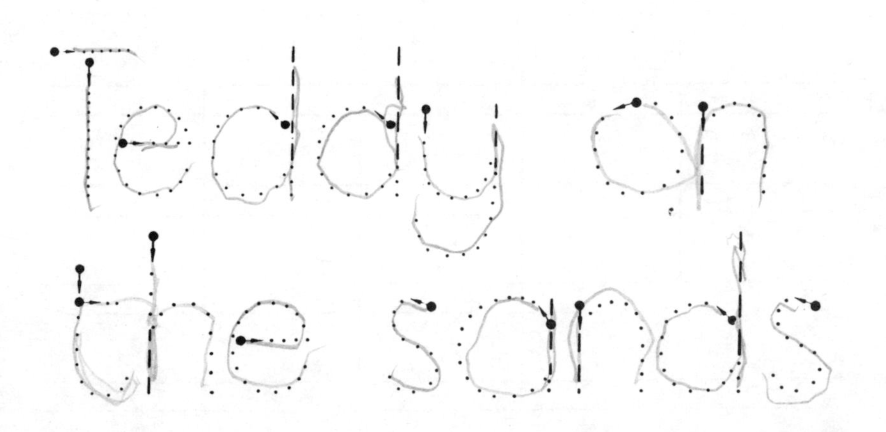

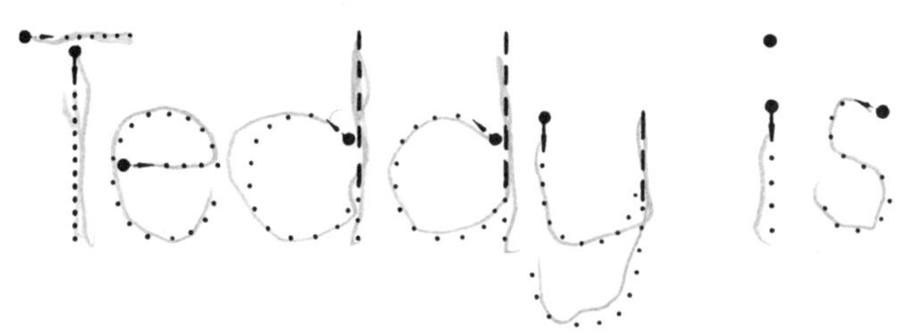
Teddy is

digging

in the

sand.

Teddy fills

his bucket
up to the
top. He
tips his
bucket of
sand top to

bottom
and
puts a
flag
on
top.

Teddy
has a
long swim.

Teddy is
very wet.

Rub,
rub,
rub!
Hurry up!

Teddy has
a lollipop.

Teddy
drinks pop
from

a can, and

drops the

empty can

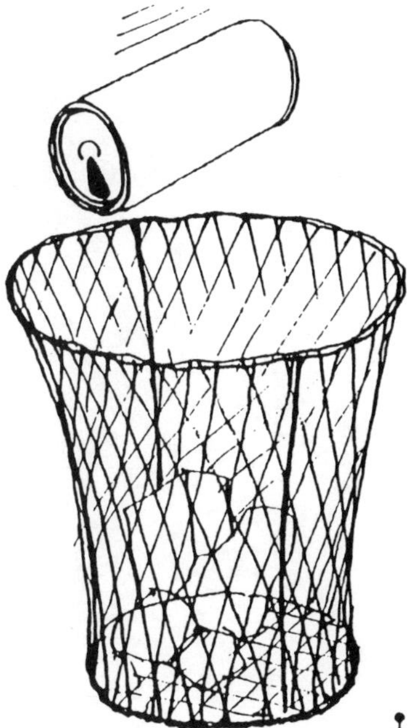

in a bin.

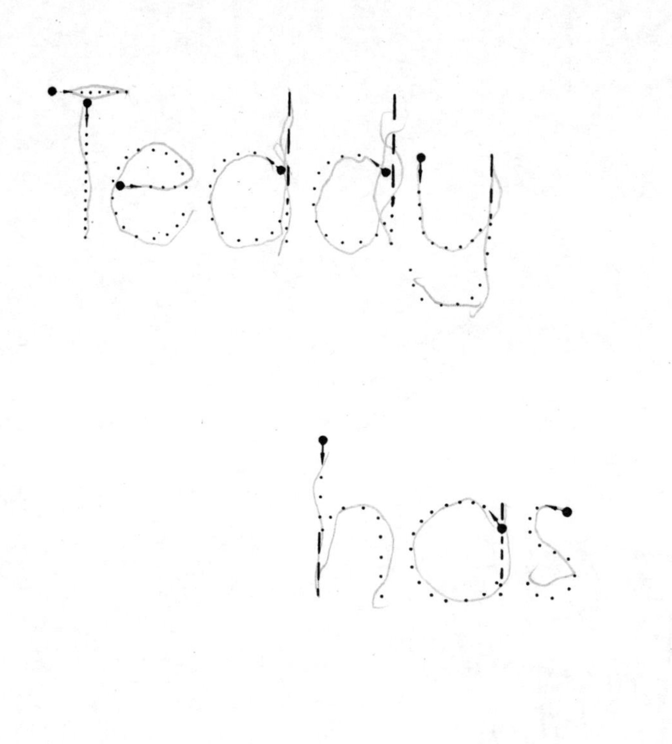
Teddy
has

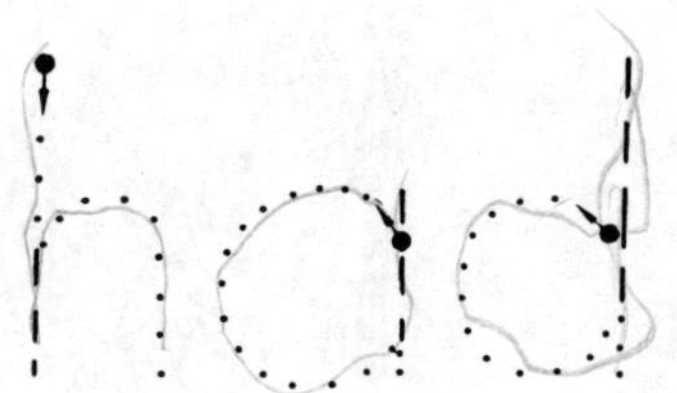
had

a
happy
day

Day 41

The next five letter-groups are vowel + r. The vowels are very important. The child can now learn the names of the vowels, which are the long sounds:

a (ay) e (ee) i (I) o (oh) u (you)

When you sing the alphabet, you are singing the names. When we sound out, we use letter-sounds, but when we talk about letters, you can now start to use their names, occasionally reminding that "aitch says h..." and so on.

ar says the sound in car, and or as in fork. Children seem to find these easier to learn than the er ir ur which all make the same sound (term, bird, curl). If you wish to go slowly, do the ar, or first and then the other three. If your child seems to be mopping it all up very easily, you can try the five together. Use your judgement.

ar: The mouth is fairly wide open for this. Try to make the r audible. The Scottish reading attainment regularly comes out better than English, and I wonder if this is due to their clearer sound of the r. Try to say carr rather than c ah. Look in the mirror, and see if your lips move forward towards the end of the sound, as they should. Exaggerate the r at the end of all five groups, for the next fortnight. Including words like 'sharp' emphasises to the pupil that letter-groups once learned keep coming in.

Day 42

Have the pupil read out the words listed:

or: The mouth is not so wide-open for this. Again, try to sound the r, so that pour/pore does not sound like paw. (I know pour is not an or word. I am just using them to draw your attention to sounds.)

Play the previous games. Sing the alphabet.

Have the pupil read the Teddy story to you.

Make the games.

ar

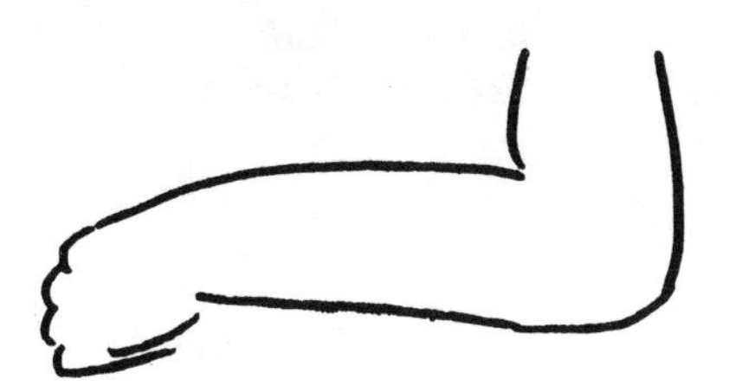

ar m
p ar k
st ar t
sh ar p
f ar m-
yar d
p ar t

f or k
st or m
sh or t
c or n
morning
n or th
c or k

Words for an ar/or bingo:

charm	spark	smart	party	hardly	depart
carpet	target	sharp	farm-yard	alarm	market
darling	north	corner	sport	lord	stork
horse	storm	morning	born	forget	cork
form	short	report	before	Gordon	Norma
porch	escort				

Day 43-45

The sounds of -er, -ir, -ur are all the same. Look in the mirror and make sure your lips come forward, side of mouth (lips) in.

-er As well as words in the list opposite, you can show how we make a comparative using -er (and a superlative).

Positive	Comparative	Superlative
fast	faster	fastest
quick	quicker	quickest
long	longer	longest
strong	stronger	strongest
rich	richer	richest

Choose your words with car. Avoid 'wet', because the t has to be doubled in wetter, wettest, and we have not yet taught doubling. Avoid wide, late, etc. becaused we have not yet taught what the e does. Avoid water because of the wa.

Just say that in many words that end in -er, the consonant in front is doubled:

hammer	spanner	better	letter
butter	slipper	pepper	grasshopper
pitter-patter			

-er is far and away the most common spelling for this sound, then ir, with ur least used. They are all easy to read, but one has to remember which you need for spelling.

Make Pairs game, bingo, and the snakes-and-ladders game.

Words for Bingo:

born	card	bird	barn	burst	charm
corner	corn	curl	dart	faster	father
fork	forty	firm	farm	fur	important
jerk	morning	murmur	nurse	person	shirt
skirt	sparkling	sport	term	thirty	thirsty
thorn	turn				

Explain that 'father' is irregular in the way we say the a.

er

fern
term
hammer
butter
faster
ladder

ir

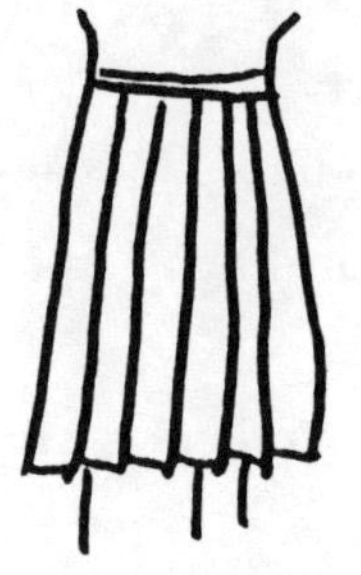

skirt
shirt
girl
bird
thirty
thirsty
firm

ur

fur
burn
turn

curl
hurt
murmur

ar	er	ir	or	ur
		bird		

Day 46-50

Your pupil may learn some sections faster than other. Adjust to this. This programme is only a guide.

The next five letter-groups are about the way the letter e works after a vowel. Your pupil has already learned that an e after e (two e's) says ee, the sound of the name of the first vowel This works for all the vowels, not just e. Thus, the first vowel says its name. The following e changes the sound of the first vowel to its name, ae (Scottish Mae), ee (see), ie (pie) oe (toe) ue (value). The pupil should now be able to say the names of the 5 vowels off pat, ay ee I oh you.

Then say: "Some rules are stronger than others. This is a very strong rule. It even works when you split the vowel and e, and put one consonant in the middle. Consonants are the 20 letters (not y) that are not the vowels."

You can teach one a day for five days, but it works very well to teach all five together, seeing how letters work.

Make the Pairs, bingo, snakes-and-ladders, Is it?

Words for bingo can include pairs like cod/code, pin/pine, fad/fade, hop/hope, even fir/fire, or can be all -e words:

cane	these	pine	toe	blue
shame	even	time	open	clue
paper	Peter	fine	over	rescue
skate	concrete	wine	rope	tube
plate	extreme	tiger	stone	fumes
game	theme	wire	those	pure
gate				excuse

The first half of the green Ridout "I Can Spell" book gives practice in these.

So that earlier leaning does not fade, it is time now to begin each lesson revising earlier work. Have the pupil read through just one column of earlier spellings, each day, and put the date at the bottom to show which ones you have done.

a.e

cake

gate
game
make
spade
skates
plate
paper
same
fade
cape
tape

see
tree

e.e

even

evening
these
theme
Steve
Crete
concrete
extreme

pie
tie

i.e

pipe

wipe
ripe
stripes
wine
time
tiger
like

toe
hoe

o.e

rose

nose
hose
those
rope
hope
stone
home

u.e

clue
rescue

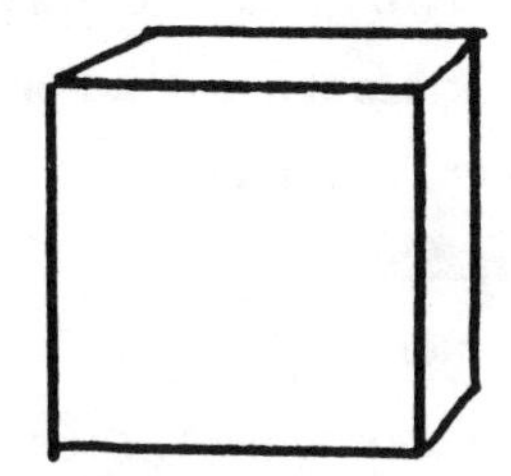

cube
tube
fumes
use
amuse
excuse
flute
computer
refuse

Day 51

Doubling

Read through this section. You may decide to leave it until later, for very young children age 3,4, but for older children and 'remedial' and adults, this section is very useful at this point as a means of making them consider letters/sounds and to stop them guessing for meaning, etc. or predicting. This emphasises that reading is all about letters, a particular sequence of letters.

'e' can "jump back over one letter" and make the vowel say its name, but cannot jump over two letters. Study:

pat/patter dip/dipper but/butter

When you want the short a to remain short, when you want to keep the sound of pat in patter, you cannot just put er after pat, because you would then have a,e. Because the vowel cannot jump back over two letters, you double the consonant in between:

bet/better, but pet/Peter

Consider comparatives ending in -er, and superlatives ending in -est.

	wide	wider	widest
	safe	safer	safest
	fine	finer	finest
but	fat	fatter	fattest
	thin	thinner	thinnest
Try:	hot	h...........	h...........
	big	b............	b............
	slim	s............	s............

When you want a double k, you put -ck-:

baker	packer	cracker	jacket	
	Becket			
wicket	cricket	ticket		
	docket	locket	socket	rocket
	bucket			

Find words for the a.e i.e and o.e in the Bingo game.

Find words for the a.e i.e and o.e in the Bingo game.

ae	tree	pie	hoe	value
	s..	t..	t..	tiss..
game	these	pile	those	tune
	P.t.r			.s.
	.v.n			am.s.
	.v.ning			exc.s.
	th.m.			c.b.
				t.b.
				f.s.
				st.d.nt
				f.m.s.
				comp.t.r

It is not just the e that can work back through a consonant and make an earlier vowel long. Any vowel can do this:

pupil/puppet acorn/accord and y works like a vowel: duty/putty navy/navvy rabid/rabbit holy/holly

but this is not a 100% rule; there are exceptions. Sometimes we can have vowel-consonant-vowel and the first vowel is short: atom, lemon, robin, but looking at it the other way, when we do have a double consonant, the vowel in front is always short:

button patter borrow marry (cf. Mary)

Because i works like e, when you add -ing, you drop the e; you do not need both.

Root word	-ing	-ed	-er
hop	hopping	hopped	hopper (-pp)
hope	hoping	hoped	hoper

Try:

strip	str.........	str.........	str.........
stripe	str.........	str.........	str.........
mat	m..........	m..........	m..........
rub	r...........	r...........	r...........
swim	s...........	s...........	s...........

Now try these: do you double the last consonant, do you drop the e, or do you make no change at all?

wipe	wi......ing	wi..........	wi..........
lick	l............	l............	l............
stop	s............	s............	s............
rust	r............	r.............	r.............
take	t............	t.............	t.............
fetch	f............	f.............	f.............
fan	f............	f.............	f.............
wish	w...........	w............	w............

Notice:

like liked liking but lick licked licking

rake raked raking but rack racked racking racket

Day 52-4

The next letter-group, -le, follows on very easily after -e and doubling. -le is the only other letter-group that does the same thing as e (or any vowel), that is, it can "jump back" over one letter, but not two, to make a vowel say its name.

Study the following. You will that the first column has a long vowel, with only one letter between the vowel and -le, whereas the second column has two letters. Those two letters can be a double letter, two different sounded letters, or -st- where the t is silent.

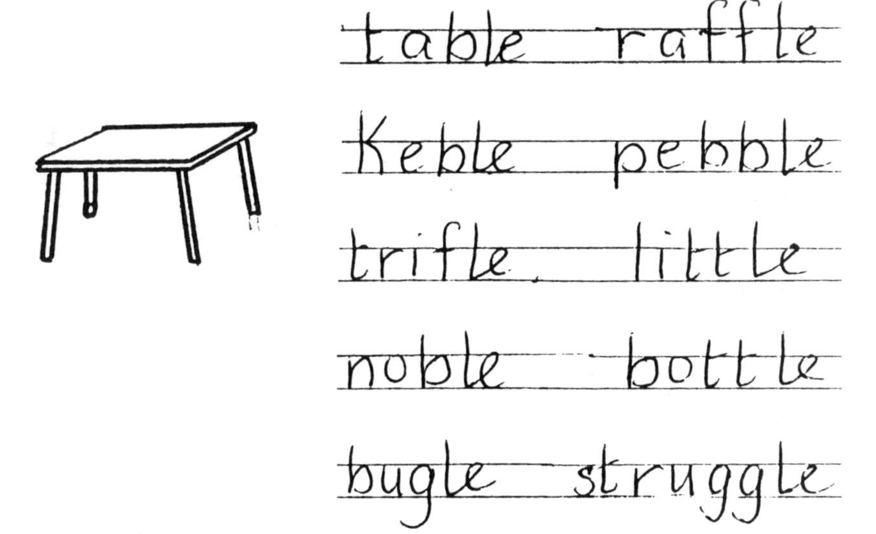

When the letters between the vowel and -le are -st-, the vowel is short and the t is silent.

When there is a c between the vowel and -le, except in the name of the town Acle, the a is short.

Long vowel ↓ le	Short ↓ le
crad	crack
cab	ripp
map	scribb
Bib	twink
id	bubb
stab	puzz
tit	jung
— st le	**BUT**
ca . . le	miracle
wre . . le	obstacle
whi . . le	oracle
jo le	spectacles
ru le	particle

In -le words, there are scores of words with the short vowel, and very few with the long vowel

Teaching how the letters work helps to keep attention on letters, sequence, direction, sounds. This stage should be short and easy. Do not wait until the pupil can spell every word. Go on when he can read the words, and play the bingo comfortably. Make and play the games.

Words for bingo:

apple	pebble	thimble	bottle	uncle
battle	settle	little		jungle
crackle	tremble	twinkle		purple
castle		whistle		cuddle
handle		simple		puzzle
		middle		struggle

Words ending in -ible and-able break the rule, the i is short: possible, terrible, visible, breakable, tolerable.

table	feeble	title	noble	bugle
		Bible		
		rifle		

Day 55

When a vowel follows another vowel, the first one usually says it name, or:

When two vowels go walking,
The first does the talking.

There are exceptions to this (break, field), but it works for oa. This is very simple., It is usually enough just to go through the list of words, or make an Is it? booklet. There is no need to make games for this.

Words: soap road float throat boat moan groan Joan foal loaf goal soak oak coat coal coast roast toast

Have the pupil repeat three times, "OA says oh!"

Say or sing the alphabet.

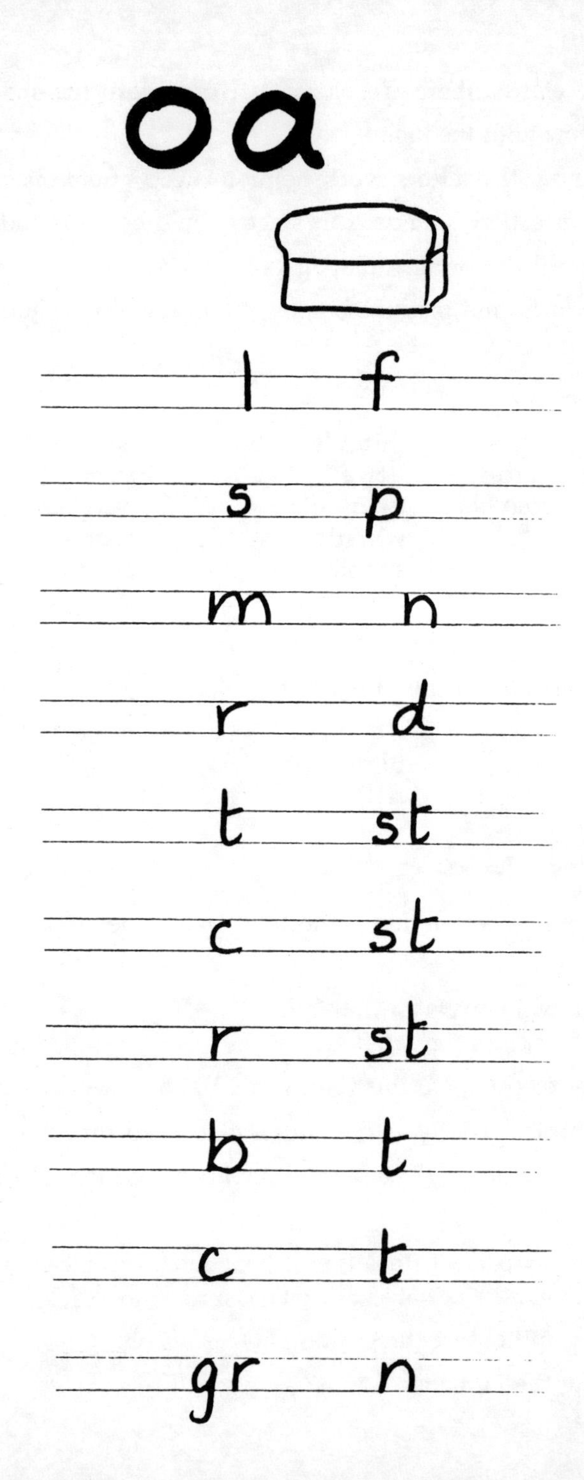
oa
l f
s p
m n
r d
t st
c st
r st
b t
c t
gr n

Read through one column of work earlier in the programme, every day, and put the date.

Sound out a longish word, and see if the pupil can complete it:

splendid	s-plendid	
	sp-lendid	
	spl-endid	
	sple-ndid	
	splen-did	
	splend-id	
	splendi-d	splendid!

Day 56-60

tray
play
pray
away
Sunday
holiday
spray
crayon

Learning one spelling rule 'unlocks' dozens of words. There is a rule:

No English word ends in q u v j or i.

This section is about the last one.

<u>ski</u> is a Norwegian word. Spaghetti, macaroni, are Italian. Taxi is half of taxicab (we say taxi, the Americans say cab). In the word I, I is the beginning, middle and end.

Thinking about this one rule, we can learn ai/ay and oi/oy at the same time as i/y.

Have the pupil say three times:

"You can't have i at the end"

then

"ai says (ay), a-y at the end".

ay-wie

"oi says oi, o-y at the end"

oh-wie

As the pupil reads through the lists of words, he must say each word, pronounce it correctly, and either know what it means, tell you if you are not sure he understands it, or he must ASK. So many children in these days of look-and-say, look and wait to be told, think that saying the word is enough, and do not ask for the meaning. This must be strongly encouraged, they must ask. Make sure they realise that asking for the meaning is a sign of intelligence and common sense, not a sign of being stupid. Indeed, it is stupid to jump over words saying them without understanding.

Make the games and <u>Is it?</u>

Words for bingo:

aim	maintain	holiday	noise	boy
chair	obtain	play	spoil	enjoy
nail	pain	Thursday	point	annoy
railway	rain	Sunday	join	oyster
entertain	train	stray	foil	
explain	strain	pray	coin	
		tray	boil	
		ray	coil	

Sing the alphabet.

Read through a column of earlier words.

Play the games.

You cannot have <u>i</u> at the end, but you can have <u>y</u> anywhere, and it can say the long or short <u>i</u> sound:

<u>Short</u>		<u>Long</u>	
funny	myth	python	dynamo
silly	pyjamas	hydrant	dynamite
family	dyslexia	satisfy	defy
system	*yes	apply	deny
syrup	yellow	multiply	qualify
pyramid	yesterday	reply	mystify

* sound as short i, not yer.

ai	ay	oi	oy
p ai nt	pl ay	b oi l	b oy
tr n	cl	f l	t
p d ← from p	p	sp l	R
l d ← from l	l	p nt	enj
s d ← from s	s	c n	ann
ag n	tr	j nt	destr
afr d	spr	t let	empl
expl n	aw	n se	.. ster
obt n	m	app nt	r.. al
m..nt..n	displ	p son	
f l	holid	av d	
n l	h		

If a word ends with y, look carefully at what happens when we add extra letters and sounds to it, after it.

happy happily happier happiest happiness

Verbs: hurry hurries hurried but hurrying (we cannot have two i's together.)

	worry	worries	w...........	w...........

and the long i sound:

	cry	cries	cried	crying
	reply	rep..........	rep........	rep..........

Nouns: pony, ponies cherry, cherries
fly, flies

You change the y into i when you add an ending. This works whether the words are verb, noun or adjective, and whether the y is long or short.

Day 61-62

Letter-groups which are consistent and reliable are easier to learn. We can say "o-a says oh!" and it will, every time. However, ea is not consistent. There are many words where ea says the same sound as ee, and many other where it says the short sound as in head. Make an Is it? book with both sounds, and tell the pupil to try the ee sound first; if that does not provide a real word, try the short e. Peas — the long ee works; steady, try steedy which is not a word so try steddy — and that is the sound.There is no rule as to which is which.

Words for the Bingo game:

please	reason	steal	deaf	bread
leave	clean	meat	ready	jealous
dear	feast	least	steady	weather
fear	breathe	near	instead	healthy
year	breach		tread	weapon
appear	easy		heavy	sweat
			dreadful	spread
			thread	feather

ea ea

sea
b ch
p ch
st m
app r

br d
h ven
h d
st dy
w th er

In four words, ear sounds like air:

bear p w t

In three words, ea sounds like ay:

break steak great

In a few words, ear sounds like er:

In heart, hearth, ear says ar.

earn
l n
ly
th

s ch
p l
h d

Day 63-69

(This may take longer.)

The pupil has by now had a lot of practice in making a c say k, and a g say its hard sound as in go; but he has also met ch saying the sound in chop. C and G are the only two letters of the alphabet that can be "hard" and "soft". The sound we learned first, as in cat, dog, is the 'hard' sound. The soft sound is the sound in their name, cee and jee, so that c sounds like sss and g sounds like j. They say this 'soft' sound when followed by e, i or y. This gives us six letter-groups:

ce ci cy ge gi gy

You can either take them one at a time, or explain the general principle and let the child try out all six, and go on from there..

When soft c,g are introduced, some children try to change every c-g into the soft sound. I say that all the words where c,g previously said the hard sound will go on saying it, that we are not changing any words we have had already, but looking at new words.

Join the two letters if you wish. This helps to imprint on the learner's mind that they go together. You will see that in the columns there are extra columns for-nce, and -age and-nge, which are common endings.

While the pupil is learning these new letter-groups, play the previous games. Make a bingo, pack of pairs card, snakes-and-ladders, and Is it? You may wish to make one Is it? for soft c and another for soft g.

This may be a good time to point out that printed material often shows

ɑ as a and ɡ as g.

These letter-groups get too little attention in workbooks. You may find in a jumble sale a copy of Royal Road Book 5 (The horse that could not run). It is very good.

Soft c.

ce	ce after long vowel	-nce
centre	face	dance
ac pt	spa	gla
pro ss	re nt	adva
suc ed	mi	Fra
ne ssary	twi	fe
ex pt	pri	differe
scar ly	gro r	ambula
as nd	o an	dista
des nd	produ r	si
par l	redu..	pri
..rtain	gra	pri ss
..ntury	la	mi r

ci	cy
city	fancy
electri ty	Nan . .
ac dent	pira . .
pen l	C ril
de de	C nthia
ex ted	. . clone
. . rcle	clamen
. . rcus	. . anide
pre ous	linder
deli ous	. . gnet (a baby swan)
s ssors	bi cle
. . nema	. . press (a tree)

ce ci

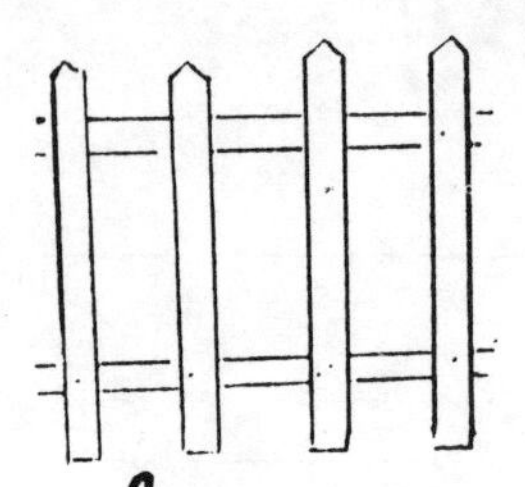

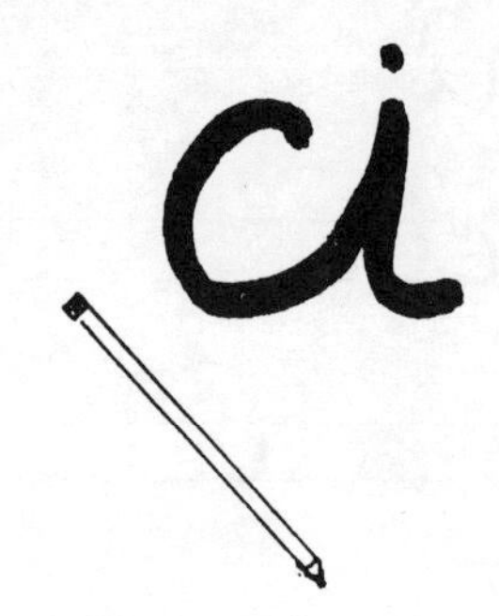

fence
dance
advance
success
necessary
December

pencil
city
accident
decide
excited
scissors

Double c: When you have a cc before a, o or u, it says k:

accost, accord, accustom.

When you have cc before e, i or y (the letters that make c soft), the first c says k and the second says s, so that cc sounds like x:

succeed	accept	accelerate
success	accent	access

Note that Dixon and Dickson sound the same.

If you can notice the "cess" in words, it helps to remember when you use c and when ss.

access   success   princess   recess   abscess   necessary

So when do you use c and when k and when ck?

ck follows a short vowel in words like

pack   peck   pick   rock   duck

The ack, eck, ick pattern is kept in packet (see p. 68).

After a long vowel, the k sound is k:

bake like stoke duke.

In a long word ending in the sound ick, it is spelt <u>ic</u>.

panic	picnic	frantic
mimic	logic	fantastic
arithmetic		

At the beginning of a word, the k sound before a, o and u is c:

cat cot cut

but before e i y it is k (because ce ci cy have the s sound):

cat		
	kettle	set
	kitten	city
cot		
cut		cycle

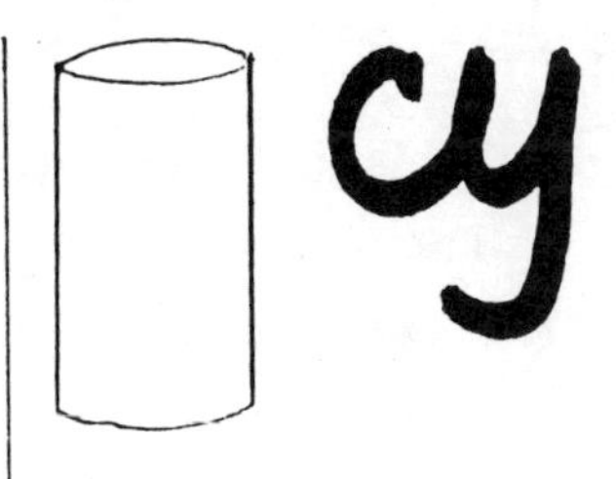

cylinder
Cyril
Cynthia
fancy
Nancy
bicycle

You see, you are learning how letters work.

By now, you may have started your pupil reading books, or you have encouraged him gradually to read more and more of the words when you read together. He is now ready to start on James Webster's "Shorty the Puppy" books, to read at one sitting, or the early Trog books (Nelson), but the child will read these so fast that it is not worth buying them, See if the school has them. If not, let him read any books with large print, just helping with words that have letter-groups not yet taught, or irregular words. Use your judgement.

Soft g

ge

My father's first name was George. All my life, until I learned the rule about ge, I wondered why his name had such an odd spelling. I learned this rule when I was 48! So you are way ahead of me!

In a word like

age
Regent
digest
Stoke Poges
huge

the first vowel has an e two letters later, so the first vowel is long. The same thing is found with ce:

face
recent
slicer
grocer
reduce

fringe
sponge
village
bandage
garage
danger

(Exception: get)

If you want a short vowel in front of ge, instead of putting two g's (except in suggest), we put -dge:

badge hedge bridge lodge smudge

This is voiced. The unvoiced equivalent is:

patch fetch witch Scotch Dutch

So, surprisingly, it is the simple

rich much such which duchess

which are irregular!

Many consonant sounds can be voiced and unvoiced, with the tongue making the same movement. A t is a lighter form of d: p/b f/v k/g (hard). The light ones we call unvoiced, and the heavier ones (d b v g (hard)) voiced. If you put hand against your throat, you can feel the tremble, vibration, with the voiced consonants.

gi

gy

engine
magic
tragic
digital
imagine
register
ginger

Exceptions: give, girl.

gymnastics
energy
allergy
biology
zoology
Egypt

-tch -dge ge

hatch	badge	gentle
scra	e	G. or ..
stre	le	lar ..
wi	sle	ur .. nt
hi	bri	wa ..
pi	sto	Re .. nt
sti	fu	di .. st
di	ju	Ni .. l
Sco	gru	co .. nt
clu	nu	hu ..
bu er	slu	
Du	bu t	suggest

-nge	-age	gi	gy
fringe	rage	gipsy	Egypt
hi	But manage	ma c	ener..
plu	vill	tra c	aller..
spo	dam	ima	ne biolo..
ora	cabb	..raffe	zoolo..
	gar	..nger	..mnastics
But change	band	..ant	
da... r	sav	re..ster	
a... l	pass	en ne	
stra... r	im	di.. tal	
ra... r	lugg		
	post		

Words for bingo:

accept	danger	face	grocer	necessary
ambulance	December	fancy	hedge	police
bicycle	decent	garage	hinge	princess
chance	digital	general	huge	register
change	excellent	giant	ice	scarcely
city	except	ginger	imagine	sponge
				suggest
				village

Note the ar in scarcely does not sound as in car, but sounds like air. This is a very difficult word.

Many words end in -nge. For e, i, o, u the vowel is short, as one would expect before two consonants:

Penge hinge fringe sponge (on sound, see later)
plunge

But a is different. In orange the a sounds like i. In other words, the a is long:

change danger stranger manger angel

Many words end in -age. The word age has a long, clear ay sound. When the -age is an ending, we do not say it as a clear age. It is a good idea to say the word with a long a the first time or two, to help with spelling:

village cabbage image bandage postage garage etc.

Day 70

If ge gi gy say je ji jy, what if we do not want this? If we want a hard g in front of e,i,y, , we must separate the ge gi gy, and we do this with a u: gu says the hard g. It forms a 'wall' between the g and the e, i, y: (See next page.)

There is a gu in guard even though not needed.

Note: regard.

gu
gu it ar
.. ess
.. est
.. ide
.. ilty
.. illot ine
..inea pig
Gu y
guard
but regard

Day 71-74

The next letter-groups to learn are based on the rule,

No English word ends in u.

Menu is French. You is the exception.

As with i/y, we can put a and o in front of u/w. If u would be at the end, we change it to a w. OU can make at least 5 sounds, OW two, but au/aw are totally consistent and make only one sound. It is surprising, therefore, that of all these sounds and spelling, it is au that usually take longest to learn.

ou

Silent o

8 x 2 = 16

double
nourish
country
cousin
famous
curious

OUR sounds like or: pour, four

OU can say oo: you youth group soup coupon route routine

OU also changes its sound in the OUGH words, see page 98.

Day 75

If we want the ou sound in cloud at the end, we must change ou to ow: but ow can say two sounds

① **ow** ②

①	②
owl	bowl
cow	snow
town	grow
crown	throw
crowd	pillow
powder	borrow
now, how	yellow

Make new games

Bingo words:

autumn	caught	flour	mouth	saucer
August	claw	ground	mountain	see-saw
automatic	cloud	haunted	outside	shower
awful	coward	jaw	paw	sound
awkward	elbow	launch	Paul	snow
because	frown	laundry	power	towels
			trousers	crowd

ou	ou	ow
out	young	cow
sh t	d ble	l
ab t	tr ble	t n
gr nd	c ple	d n
s nd	c ntry	dr n
p nd	c sin	p der
s th	n rish	sh er
m th	enc rage	fl er
h se		cr d
m se		t el
tr sers		cl n
c nt		t er

ow	au	aw
snow	Paul	paw
gr..	A.. gust	j..
sh	l nch	cl..
thr	l ndry	l.. n
m er	h nted	.. ful
pill..	.. thor	.. kward
yell..	.. tomatic	y.. n
sorr..	.. tumn	str..
bl	f lt	dr..
arr	.. dience	s..
fl	bec se	l..
borr	s cer	sh l

Day 76, 77

au **aw**

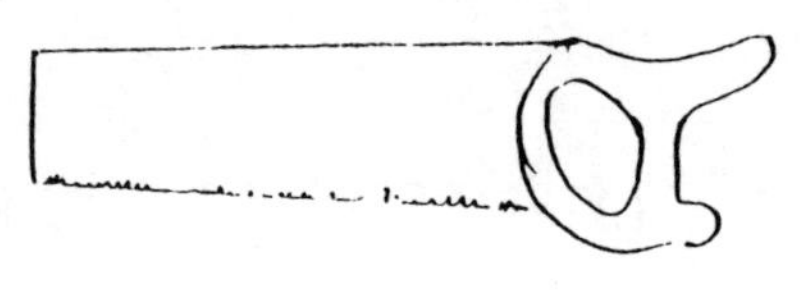

Paul
August
haunted
automatic
because
launch
laundry

saw
paw
claw
lawn
yawn
straw
outlaw
crawl

Day 78 gh, ght

Our beautiful language is made up of words from many other languages. When the Vikings came over, their language contained a sound in the back of your throat, a guttural that the Anglo-Saxons could not pronounce, so they got round it either by leaving out the gh (as in light) or by putting in another sound, and they did not even keep to one sound! In -ght words (and others), the gh has Gone Home:

light

s______

f______

br______

n______

t______

fl______

fr______

m______

r______

Note: sigh
high
eight
weight
weigh
neigh
sleigh

OUGHT sounds the same as AUGHT:

ought	caught
bought	taught
brought	daughter
fought	slaughter
thought	
nought	BUT laugh, laughter.

Day 79-80

See next page. Have the pupil repeat over and over just the four letters "O...U...G...H" (their names, not sounds) not "o-u-gh- says..." because the sound keeps changing. The words should be read down, first with the help of pronunciation clues, then from bottom to top, then random, then try to spell them, dictated.

-ough

In cough
trough
the ough says OFF

en....
r....
t....
UFF

pl
b
ow as in cow

thr
oo

d
alth
oh!

thor ly
bor
u as in cup

Day 81

Wa hardly ever says the sound in wax, waggle. It sounds like wo; qua (except in quack) sounds like quo. War sounds like wor, and wor sounds like wer. By now, just completing words in a column (pronounce correctly, know what it means, or ask) is sufficient to deal with the remaining letter-groups. Continue to play the old games, read through one early letter-group column each day.

was	quarrel	warm
. . nt	. . rry	ning
. . sh	lity	. . . den
h . t	. . ntity	s . . m
tch	s . . sh	re . . . d
sp	s . . bble	back . . d
. . ffle	s . . dron	quart
nd	. . rantine	. . . ter
s . . n		. . . tz
s . . llow		

Day 82

Al often says aw

Wor says wer.

all	walk	word
ball	t k	ld
c	ch k	m
t	st k	k
st	F kland	th
sm	halt (Sound l)	se
h	m t	st
f	s t	also
w	b d	most
	sc d	ways
		together

Day 83

In words that come from French, -ine as an ending sounds like -een, and -ique sounds like eek. Endings que and gue sound like k and (hard) g.

mach**ine**	che**que**
Paul	anti
mar	uni
marger	pictures
guillot	grotes . . .
magaz	catalo**gue**
tanger	dialo
nectar	fati
strychn	intri
chlor	lea . . .
trampol	ro . . .

Day 84

The sound of ū

blue	cube	music	suit
cl	t b	p. pil	fr t
gl	t n	.niform	recr t
c	f m s	. nion	br. . se
val	c r	. niversity	cr . . se
tiss	ac t .	h. mid	j . . ce
stat	st d . nt	. s . al	
resc	am . s .	grad . al	
aven	exc . s	pec . liar	
que	comp t r	t . lip	
		d . ty	
		st . pid	

Day 85

new

f

Another language from which we get many words is Greek. In these words, ph says f, and ch says k.

bl (blow) | dolphin | school
gr (grow) | ele ant | e o
thr (throw) | or an | emist
ch | ilip | an or
st | tele one | ristmas
scr | al abet | orus
st ard | ne ew | Ni olas
vi | otogra | aracter
 | antom | stoma -
 | easant | a e

Day 86

The thick black letter is silent.

knife	wrong	climb
. night	. rist	com .
.. ow	wr eck	clim . ed
.. ew	.. en	. com . ed
ob	.. estle	lam .
ot	. eath	lim .
it	.. ap	dum . (cannot hear)
ee	.. ing (twist)	crum .
eel	. inkle	thum .
ock	. ite	
uckle	Norwich	yolk
	answer	folk

Day 87

hymn but hymnal
=sounded

autum. autumnal

solem solemnity

colum columnar

sign, but signal, signature.

hour gnash

.onest .nu

.onour .nat

g.ost .naw

psalm .nome

pa.m

ca.m

Day 88

In a very few words, 'ti' says sh, which is very strange. In many, many words 'on' says un; it hardly ever says the sound in 'on'. If you put ti before on, you have -tion which is an ending and sounds like 'shun'. In these words the stress is usually on the syllable before the -tion. There are hundreds of words like this. Many words end in -ation, and in these words the a is long and has the stress. "Stress" means more emphasis, spoken on a higher note than the other syllables.

ti = sh	on = un	tion = shun
pa**ti**ent	w**on**	suc**tion**
cau ous	s	ac....
ini al	d e	men....
essen al	fr t	atten....
confiden.al	..i..	inven....
influen..al	L..d..	inspec
iner..a	pers.	prescrip
pruden.al	m..th	addi

Day 89

- ā tion	- ture says cher
station	capture
sens	adven
decor	mix
inform	fix
educ	pic
consider	punc
convers	fu
ventil	furni
popul	na
associ	lec
separ	scrip
examin	crea

Day 90

ie usually says the long sound: pie, tie, cried. It can see ee:

field	chief	priest
yield	grief, grieve	piece (a piece of pie)
shield	relief, relieve	
	belief, believe	

There is a rule: "i before e except after c::

ceiling	Exceptions:	neither
receive		foreign
deceive		their
conceit		leisure
		seize
	and a few more.	

ei sometimes says ay:

vein	weigh
veil	neigh
reign	sleigh
eight	neighbour
weight	reindeer

Day 91

Many words begin with be- re- de-. If you get used to this, you will sound out 'begin' correctly, and not be put off by sounding 'beg...in'

begin	refresh	decay
..hind	..mind	..lay
..come	..fuse	..fy
..cause	..gret	..fend
..long	..member	..sire
..have (long a)	..alise	..pend
..lieve	..sult	..clare

and many more

By now reading will be safe. There are still rules to learn, but for most children this foundation is more than enough. What is today's date? Check to see how many days it did take you. If you would take the time, I would be most grateful if you would let me know, giving also the age when your child started on this programme.

You now know what "teaching reading" is. You will wonder how anybody ever believed the silly theories! and why they go on. Perhaps you would show this book to the infant teacher at your local school? Today's failure is needless, and a programme like this is the way to prevent it.

If you want further work along these lines, "Alpha to Omega" by B. Hornsby and F. Shear (Heinemann Educational) is excellent. There are workbooks which are quite good, but they are not systematically graded as this book is, but now that you know the rules, it does not matter if the workbook hops about in its programnme. You could try the remaining books of Ridout's "Now I Can Spell" (Collins), and Spell Well books 1-5 by Henderson (Blackie), and "Moving on with Reading", J. Hughes (Nelson).

If you can keep your child supplied with plenty of books, let him choose his own from the local library, and make reading a family activity, you will have given your child a lifetime of pleasure and, I hope, enjoyed doing so.

MONA McNEE
2 THE CRESCENT
TOFTWOOD
EAST DEREHAM
NORFOLK NR19 1NR

We do not need new teachers, but we do need new teaching — or rather, we need to go back to the old teaching set out in this book. The new teaching is all based on ideas and opinions, not on facts or properly tested and monitored changes. The silly ideas are so wrong, they have been around for so long and believed by so many that the sheer size of the problem, its enormity protects it! People cannot believe it is that bad. They feel "They'd never allow it", so they go on trusting the experts. They assume, students and others that the professors know what they are doing. Well — we have 6 million illiterates, and unless the National Curriculum is either withdrawn, or given a firm foundation in intensive systematic phonics, this number will increase.

The taxes now being gobbled up by education are no longer value-for-money, because of the amount of reading failure, total or partial. If you cannot read, secondary school life is a prison sentence. Illiteracy is a prison.

So what have the teachers been told? — and believed.

The myths

1. "Phonics is old-fashioned, dull as ditchwater" You who have watched your child learning from this book and the games will know that phonics need not be dulll. The main thing is that it works. Nothing is more boring than failure.

"Reading is so much more than just saying the words," they say. True — but if you can say the word, you are far better off than if you can NOT say the word. And for all the words already in our spoken and understood vocabulary, being able to say the word gives you access to the meaning. Those trying to mock phonics out of existence try to imply that when you read a word by phonics, you do not understand it. This is not true and they have no grounds for saying it.

2."We should read words as wholes, as word-shapes. Can you read these words from their shape?

They are three different ways of writing a word-shape. The teachers who require children to read before knowing letters have never tried to read words without letters. It is impossible. These words are: average, sixpence (the shape is formed by what Americans call blocking), and apparent, a kind of skeleton. The shape for "average" could also be revenge, manage.

Many words fit the same shape. If we could read words from their shape, and if this were in some way better than having letters, books would be printed in word-shapes. A tree, a fish, a table, these things are wholes, and are the same no matter from which end you view them, but words, like figures and music, are a sequence — of letters. If you change one letter, you have a different word. You cannot analyse a whole.

The National Curriculum recommends word-shapes. It devotes 677 words to non-phonics, "language experience" and the like. The child is supposed to be plunged straight into "rich and stimulating texts" before he knows a single letter. The National Curriculum gives only two words "phonic cues", to hinting that we should teach children HOW to read, and never mentions the alphabet.

If there are only a few, say 20, words, a child can remember that "aeroplane" is the longest, and "is" has a dot on top, but as the number of words mounts up, the child can no longer tell one from the others. The teacher nevertheless often thinks the child is reading, because (unable to read) he resorts to other 'strategies'. He guess from the picture. He learns book after book off by heart. He guesses from the first letter — or a combination of many cues which are approved in the National Curriculum. It is at age 7 that many parents realise their child is not really reading, that while he may "read" a story, he cannot read a separate word on its own, and by that time

a) two precious years have been lost;

b) the child has probably lost confidence;

c) he has gained aquite erroneous idea of what reading actually is. He thinks you really can guess, and that an approximation is near enough. He has never developed the automatic habit of going through the letters left to right. As a result of years of this, 18-year-olds in America misread:

Printed word	Read as
delicacy	delinquency
bivouac	bifocals
timid	diminished
bos'n	cow
God knows	good news
neurosurgeon	trapeze

You see, if children are not taught HOW to read, they are lost.

3. "Guessing is OK"

It is breath-taking that teachers should ever have given up on accuracy. A child reads "home" as "house", but it is not a house, it is a flat. If the printed word is "pony" and the child reads it as "horse", does this really not matter? Anyway, if nothing else, this should ring every alarm bell in the town that the child cannot read, because "horse" does not start with a p.

4. "Reading from pictures is OK." We do not read from pictures. We read from print and nowhere else. Again, resorting to pictures is a danger signal, yet the National Curriculum recommends it.

5. "The best way you can help your child is to read to and with him." There are some children who may learn to read thus, but they are the children who will learn any way, and will not be harmed by this book. For most children, reading if done at the speed for it to carry any meaning , is far too fast for the infant to identify, study and learn individual letters, not to mention the letter-groups when the sound changes (sh does not say s...h...).

Teaching a child how to read, learning to read, is simply a different activity from "reading", just as learning to drive a car, or play the piano, or do arithmetic, is not the same for a beginner as for an expert. We must first learn HOW.

Many theories, notably those of Frank Smith, have been derived from a study of fluent readers, and this is why they are wrong.

6. "The teacher is the most important factor."

This is perhaps the most widely believed myth of all. If it were true, then with so many hard-working, well-meaning teachers, all would be well. But over and over again, world-wide, the same teachers, just by dropping the whole-word teaching, have seen attainment rise by the same amount, not just a bit but enormously (one standard deviation). No matter how "good" and dedicated a teacher is, she cannot make a "dead wrong" method work. Teacher, child, parents, all get frustrated.

7. "Johnny isn't ready".

Most children are ready to start by age 4, some even earlier, if they start on phonics. If you try to start them on whole-word teaching, they cannot. Instead of taking them off whole-word teaching at once, the teachers have been trained to wait, and they tell parents, "Don't worry. He'll catch on." Six million didn't.

8. Low I.Q. "Johnny is so stupid that it will take him a long time to learn. He will be a slow-learner."

I doubt this. My son Tim has Down's syndrome. He was my first pupil. He taught me how to teach reading. I was told his I.Q. was 65. Specially qualified teachers let him sit two years with Ladybird Book 2. When I started teaching him myself — untrained, desperate — using simple phonics, he went steadily through the Royal Road scheme, which has a fairly steep gradient, and progress never halted. 18 months later he could read — and I had to tell the school! So I believe, "If he could, they all can" — unless severely put off by wrong teaching.

Moreover, on this I think the experts will in time be proved doubly wrong, not that low I.Q. stops a child learning, but that not learning to read prevents the normal development of I.Q.!

Consider the following:

Boy age 6.2*, could not read, I.Q. 97.
10 months later, age 7.0 but with Reading Age 9.0, his I.Q. had risen to 118, and a year later had gone up another 9 points: Total rise 30 points.

Boy age 7.6, could not read, I.Q. 82, 9 months later had a reading age of 7.8 and I.Q. had risen 24 points.

Boy age 8.8, R.A. 6.9, I.Q. 108; 8 months later, C.A. 9.4, R.A. 9.0, I.Q. rise of 22 points.

Girl age 5.8, could not read, I.Q. 92.
19 months later, C.A. 7.4, R.A. 9.6, I.Q. rise 50 points.

and conversely

Boy age 7.0, R.A. 6.6, I.Q. 120, in 2.8 years only improved his reading by 1 year, i.e. the gap widened, and I.Q. fell to 113, a drop of 7 points.

We need a large-scale check on this, but does not fit in with low I.Q. as a cause of reading failure.

* C.A. is chronological age.

9. "Schools need more money."

When we drop the wrong teaching, phonic teaching is far cheaper than the long-drawn-out schemes. We shall save all the £millions now needed for remedial. Attainment will rocket while cost drops to a fifth or even less, of today's spending. We shall probably need to spend less on truancy and other social ills, and YTS.

10. "We do teach phonics."

Very few schools teach intensive, systematic phonics-first. Many teacher do not know what the spelling rules are. What they claim as phonics is usually too little, too late and poor quality, such as deductive phonics:

If BUT BETTER BASKET all start with the sound of 'b', then this shape at the beginning must be what says 'b'. It is a b (bee).

The children are expected to learn a lot of words by sight and from them work out the connection between letters and sounds. This puts the cart before the horse.

Because teachers do not know the spelling rules, some of them say "English is not phonetic" as a reason not to teach phonics. One telephone caller asked me how I would sound out "church". Did he expect me to give 6 sounds for 6 letters? But we sound church as

ch ur ch

Another secondary teacher asked the same question about "chemist", not knowing that in words from the Greek language ch says k (echo, school, Christmas etc)

The Republican statement (see page 119) is right in saying that "reading experts' lack of knowledge about phonic teaching" is one of the obstacles to reading reform.

11. "Blame the victim" When children fail, teachers (as students) are trained to look for the cause in home/child/family. This is clearly the best way to keep the blame off the teaching,

12. "No one way to teach reading." Either you start at the beginning with letters, or you start with some larger unit which is not letters. Starting with words, sentences, books, is simply not safe for at least 10% of the population, so that leaves phonics, starting with letters/sounds as the only safe way. So far from there being no one way,

THERE IS ONLY ONE SAFE WAY.

When you drop whole-word teaching, attainment rises not just for dyslexics, but right across the board:

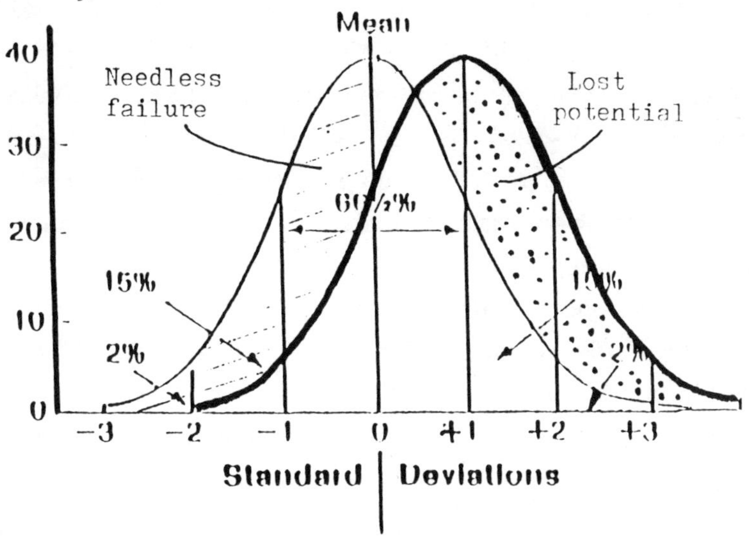

Closely connected with "No one way" is "All children are different," that what suits one child may not suit the next. The old way suited all, and still does. Only when they introduced a harmful

start, look-say, did the many "ways" begin to appear. We heard, "Don't interfere. Using two methods will confuse." Now they say, "We use all methods." The gospel changes over time, but at any one time it is presented as fact.

"All children are different" is half of the truth, but it throws out of the window any possibility of standards and minimum expectations. It let in ideas like "Horses for courses", that what suits one child will not suit the next — this was never tested. It helped to explain why for some children the new method did not work, after they had dropped the safe method.

It is the justification for having an individual programme for each child — they say. In practice, each child gets the same introduction and merely proceeds at a different pace. Class teaching means that all children are kept together, a principle like a sheepdog keeping all the sheep going the right way, and fast sheep can race ahead so long as they head the right way. Class teaching gives 30 times more, 3000% more, teacher-pupil contact, which is another reason for faster progress. Class teaching also allows the teacher then to say, "Now get on with it" reading or writing on their own while she can attend properly to the slower ones. Class teaching works because the other half of the truth is: "All children have common needs."

The Progressives tried to equalise downwards, thinking that when they got rid of the elite (and you never will), the rest would stay put. What happened? When the top band came down, so did all the rest. The gap between top and bottom is now wider than ever. What manner of people can be so dark of soul as to want to eradicate excellence? We must expand the elite until 90% of us are elite — and with the power of TV this is within our grasp. Spared look-say, the council estates of 1950 would by now be the new stockbroker belts. Look-say is the biggest single factor in our social disintegration.

Intensive, systematic phonics is the ladder out of the pit. Illiteracy is a prison sentence, a life sentence.

DYSLEXIA

Dyslexia affects at least 1 child in ten, and four boys are affected to every 1 girl.

It is an inborn, latent potential to muddlement, as far as reading and spelling are concerned, and it is usually activated by starting with whole words. Intensive, systematic phonics is the the help which dyslexics need. If they started on phonics, and were spared whole-word teaching, 29 out of 30 would learn to read and spell along with the rest of us, and 90% of the population would spell better. The failure is created, needlessly. It is whole-word teaching that makes most dyslexics word-blind.

When drug companies sold Thalidomide, they had to pay compensation to the deformed babies. It is curious that (so far) wrong teaching seems able to escape claims for damages.

Whole-word teaching is the Thalidomide of education. When it stops, attainment rockets. It goes under many names: look-say, sentence method, paired reading, shared reading, apprenticeship, "real books", whole language. One must ask why the harm it does is never identified by H. M. Inspectors, N.F.E.R etc., and why the National Curriculum embraces the wrong teaching.

Children should learn to read in two years or less. Children over 7 should not need to be taught reading. Until we get infant teaching put right, all teachers will be fed up, and secondary education a non-event for many. We are losing so much human potential, a brain-drain far exceeding that of graduates going to America. This disaster is world-wide in all English-speaking countries. America has 27m illiterates.

The modern teaching in America in "dead wrong", says a statement made on 13.9.89 by the U.S. Senate Republican Policy Committee, and that "dead wrong" teaching is what the National Curriculum

Committee, and that "dead wrong" teaching is what the National Curriculum recommends here. You would think that statement would be headline news, but it has not broken through to the British public, except by(a) the Eastern Evening News, Norwich, and (b) the Daily Telegraph Nov 30th 1989.

Among obstacles to reform it lists factors which apply equally here:

* refusal of reading experts to accept outside criticism;
* reading experts' lack of knowledge about phonics teaching;
* unsubstantiated information in educational publications
* refusal to admit that there is a literacy crisis;
* lack of legal redress for malpractice in reading instruction;
* establishment of... teacher education as a monopoly.

It concludes:

"The overwhelming evidence from research and classroom results indicates that the cure for the "disease of illiteracy" is the restoration of the instructional practice of intensive, systematic phonics in every primary school in America!"

The State of Ohio passed a law requiring this, in October 1989, a world 'first'. Ohio children will have intensive phonics from Kindergarten to Third Grade, the 4 years of our First Schools. Unless other states copy quickly, Ohio will be far ahead of national average two years from now.

When we drop the whole-word idea and go back to phonics first, this will gradually work through and transform our entire education system. Nothing else will do this. Learning to read is fundamental, and very simple. Until teachers do it, parents must. School governors should press for a return to phonics and an end of whole-word teaching. They should keep track of failure and its cost.

Last year H. M. Inspectors visited 17 schools and reported that two using phonics did well, one with an hour a week of phonics producing children who were free readers in two years — even the low attainers. In general these schools were reaching this stage in SIX years — but still the H. M. Inspectors said that the teaching of reading generally was "at least" satisfactory! If one school can teach reading in 2 years, how can it be satisfactory to take six years?

Just imagine the attainment if all children had an hour a day of phonics! The harm done by whole-word teaching is beyond belief. The spin-off affects whole-life job prospects, income, limited leisure pursuits, frustration, humiliation, truancy etc. The only factor, of many investigated among delinquents in America, that correlated with aggression was reading failure. Is literacy the cure for football violence? TV reports on truancy, football problems etc., never mention literacy, the reading age at 7 of the disruptive teenagers.

So teach your own child, the time-honoured, simple, safe way: intensive, systematic phonics. Seeing your child learn to read is one of the joys of parenthood, and many can do this before school age.

Have fun!

— — — — —

The cheapest, fastest way to tackle illiteracy nationally is via TV. A year-long series, a weekly lesson of about half an hour repeated daily, would reach all — parents, pre-schoolers, infants, remedial, dyslexics, delinquents, adult illiterates and semi-literates, truants, prisoners, gipsies. Because the programmes supposed to tackle illiteracy derive from the whole-word idea, perhaps 6 or 10 words "taught" at top speed each week, they will not work. It is cruel to have programmes to convince the illiterate how important reading is. He knows it better than we do. What he needs is access to intensive, systematic phonics. Much of the Adult Literacy (ALBSU) "help" is "language experience". Oh for the good old days of

c...a...t : cat!

General books (* contain a phonic programme)

"Reading, writing and speech problems in children"
Samuel T. Orton, 1937 (Pub.: W.W. Norton, N.Y.)
* "Why Johnny Can't Read" Rudolf Flesch, 1955. (Harper, Row)
"Why Johnny STILL Can't Read" Rudolf Flesch 1981 (Harper, Row)
"Reading: Chaos and Cure" Terman & Walcutt, 1958 (McGraw Hill)
"Preventing Failure in the primary grades" 1969
S. Engelman (S.R.A. Chicago)
"The Psychology of Reading" Gibson & Levin, 1975 (M.I.T.)
Books by:
Jeanne Chall, Diane Ravitch, Denis Stott.
"Preventing Reading Failure" P. Groff 1987
(National Book Co., U.S.A.)
"The Great American Reading Machine"
D. Yarington 1978 (Hayden Book Co., N. J.)
* "The New Illiterates" S. Blumenfeld 1973, 1988
(Paradigm Co., Boise, Idaho)
"N.E.A.: Trojan Horse in American Education"
S. Blumenfeld 1984 (Paradigm Co.)
"Illiteracy in America" 1986 National Advisory Council on Adult Education (Govt. Printer, Washington D. C.)
* "The Writing Road to Reading"
Spalding & Spalding 1957 on (W. Morrow & Co.)

Helpful teaching books, schemes, materials

ATTACK Jean Richards, Reeve Hall, Hepworth, Diss IP22 2PP
"Letterland" Lyn Wendon, Nelson
Distar S.R.A. Newtown Road, Henley on Thames RG9 1EW
METRA Educational Technology Consultants, 1 Beechwood Ave.
Ryton, Tyne & Wear, NE40 3LX
Programmed Reading Kit, D. Stott
"Alpha to Omega" Hornsby & Shear Heinemann Educational
"Teach your child to read properly!" N. Madsen, Elliot Right Way
"The First Reading & Writing Book" Mgt. Hooton,
Heinemann Educational.
"The Second Reading & Writing Book, Mgt. Hooton,
Heinemann Educational.

Books promoting the fashionable methods

Authors: W. Bloom, Y and K. Goodman, M. Meek, R. Pinder,
Frank Smith, Liz Waterland, and many others.

Books about dyslexia

"Understanding dyslexia" 1974 on, T.R. Miles
(Hodder & Stoughton, Teach Yourself)
"Overcoming dyslexia" Beve Hornsby, 1988 (Futura)
"This book doesn't make cens sens..." J. Augur 1981
"Reversals" autobiography of Eileen Simpson , 1980 (Gollancz)
"Susan's Story" autobiography of Susan Hampshire 1983 (Sphere)
"Reading and the Dyslexic Child" R.M.N. Crosby 1976, 1983
(Souvenir Press)
"Dyslexia" Goldberg & Schiffman 1972

Rule of thumb: I have found that the useful books are written in simple English, and books with a lot of polysyllables too often re-hash previous authors.

— — — — —

This book is not comprehensive. It provides enough intensive, systematic phonics for most children to learn to read. For further work, see "Alpha to Omega", and try a workbook series such as:

Spell Well Workbooks 1 - 5, by Henderson (Blackie)

Moving on with Reading 1 - 5 by John Hughes (Nelson)

or for younger children the series already mentioned:

"Now I Can Spell" 1 - 8 Ridout (Collins)

Sounds, Words and Pictures by John Hughes (Nelson)

Sounds in Sentences by John Hughes (Nelson)

Keystones by John Hughes (Nelson)

"Sure-fire Phonics" A. Williams & J. Rogerson (Nelson)

Spelling, Books 0 - 8 J. Smith (Cassell)

"Say, Write and Spell" E. W. Ellis (Stanley Thornes)

THE READING REFORM FOUNDATION

In 1955 Rudolf Flesch exposed the look-say "Method" of teaching reading as a fraud and disaster. Shortly afterwards, supporters of look-say set up in America what they called the International Reading Association. Combined with teacher trainers, and the publishers of look-say reading schemes, the I.R.A. has advocated and defended look-say ever since. As a result, America now has 27m illiterates and we have 6 million.

To challenge the look-say lobby, the Reading Reform Foundation was set up in America in 1961, and has helped many thousands of people to learn to read. They were a powerful force in contributing to the study which led to the Republican statement mentioned earlier, and probably as a result of that, the new Ohio law mandating phonics. It took 28 years. That is some indication of the strength of the look-say lobby, which operates here equally. At least in America books against look-say do get published. Here student teachers have little chance of hearing about the harm done by look-say.

In September 1989, Mona McNee decided to set up a badly-needed U.K. Chapter of the R. R. F. and to this end spent a week in Tacoma, on the West coast of America, studying the work of the R.R.F. and meeting Marion and Paul Hinds. The U. K. Chapter is now in existence and growing rapidly. It needs massive membership, in order to challenge the Department of Education and the teacher-training centres.

The R. R. F. publishes a newletter 6 times a year. If you would like to receive this, send £3 to Mona McNee, 2 The Crescent, Toftwood, East Dereham NR19 1NR.

Form your own local group. Talk to other people. Britain can get back on its feet, and the first step is literacy.